WILD ABOUT LITERACY

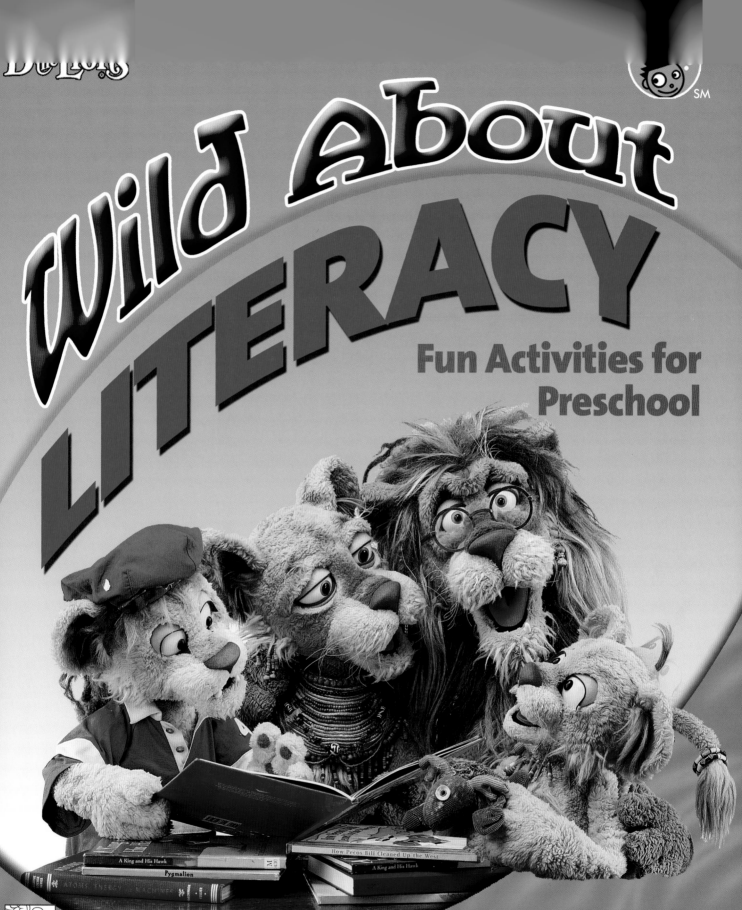

Wild About

LITERACY

Fun Activities for Preschool

by the *Between the Lions*® Staff

Based on the Award-Winning PBS KIDS® Literacy Series

Gryphon House

BETWEEN THE LIONS is produced by WGBH Boston, Sirius Thinking, Ltd., and Mississippi Public Broadcasting.

BETWEEN THE LIONS is funded in part by The Corporation for Public Broadcasting, a cooperative agreement from the U.S. Department of Education's Ready To Learn grant, and by the Barksdale Reading Institute. National corporate funding is provided by Chick-fil-A, Inc.

Visit us on the Web at: pbskids.org/lions

Printed in China through Asia Pacific Offset, April 2010. This product conforms to CPSIA 2008.

Published by Gryphon House, Inc.
10770 Columbia Pike, Suite 201
Silver Spring, MD 20901
301.595.9500
301.595.0051 (fax)
800.638.0928 (toll-free)

Visit us on the web at www.gryphonhouse.com

© Photographs by WBGH Educational Foundation and Sirius Thinking, Ltd. All rights reserved *or* by ©iStockphoto LP 2009. All rights reserved. www.istockphoto.com.

Library of Congress Cataloging-in-Publication Data
Wild about literacy / by the Between the Lions staff.
    p. cm.
 ISBN 978-0-87659-306-6
1. Language arts (Preschool)--Activity programs. I. Between the lions (Television program)
 LB1140.5.L3W55 2010
 372.6--dc22
                                                            2010012433

Table of Contents

Introduction

Between the Lions is an award-winning children's television series named for a family of lions—Theo, Cleo, Lionel, and Leona—who run a library like no other. The doors "between the lions" swing open to reveal a place in which characters pop off the pages of books, letters sing, and words come alive.

This book, *Wild About Literacy,* is a unique educational resource by the same people who created *Between the Lions*. You can use the activities and ideas in the book to teach key literacy skills to individual children or small groups of children to help them build a strong foundation in early literacy. The chapters in this book follow The Literacy Scope and Sequence (see pages 14–15), which was developed by the staff of *Between the Lions* and is aligned with state preschool standards as well as national Head Start frameworks.

This introduction provides an overview of *Wild About Literacy*, the literacy scope and sequence used in the book, a checklist to help you set up your classroom, as well as a glossary that explains the meaning of important literacy terms.

Overview of Wild About Literacy

Wild About Literacy has eight chapters with more than 150 activities. Each chapter focuses on one component of literacy in The Literacy Scope and Sequence, which is described and defined in this introduction. The activities in each chapter are grouped by topic and then by age (3+ or 4+) within each topic. The activities have the following components:

> Skill Focus
> Theme Connection(s)
> Vocabulary
> Materials
> Preparation (if necessary)
> What to Do

Skill Focus—lists the literacy skills that the activity addresses and other skills that young children need to learn, such as fine motor skills or emotional awareness.

Look for Click the Mouse!
Click the Mouse is a character on the award-winning show *Between the Lions*. When she appears on the show, something remarkable happens! Click the Mouse and the website address of pbskids.org/lions/gryphonhouse appear on many pages of *Wild About Literacy* followed by a list of stories, poems, songs, video clips, and/or games that complement the activity on that page and enhance your work in the classroom. Share this website with the children's families so they can use the stories, songs, poems, video clips, and games to support what their children are learning in your classroom.

Theme Connections—lists one or two familiar early childhood themes that the activity covers.

Vocabulary—lists words that are part of the activity. Use these when you are engaging children in the activity, defining their meaning if necessary. Repeat these words throughout the day so children hear the words used in context and can begin to understand how each word is used.

Materials—lists, in alphabetical order, the materials you will need to do the activity. Be sure you have the materials you need before you begin the activity.

Preparation—If the activity needs any preparation, such as writing a song or poem on chart paper or preparing a chart, what you need to do is described in this section.

What to Do—Step by step, this section outlines how to engage children in the activity.

In addition, many activities include ideas that build on the main activity, extend it to another curriculum area, or suggest books that relate to the activity.

The Building Blocks of Literacy

It is essential that all children develop these building blocks of literacy. Each component is described below and then presented in chart form on pages 14–15.

Oral Language: Listening and Speaking

Research tells us that before children become readers, they need to listen and talk a lot. Keep your classroom alive with the sounds of children talking, singing, and playing with the sounds in words. Have conversations with children about topics that interest them, introducing new words and concepts and inviting children to talk about their lives. Throughout the day, create opportunities for children to listen to environmental sounds, music, songs, poems, chants, and stories. Focused talk around listening activities builds children's listening and speaking vocabulary.

Book Appreciation and Knowledge

Love of books and the joys of reading are at the heart of a successful literacy program. Children enjoy many different kinds of books, including folktales, rhyming books, alphabet books, and concept books. Include a variety of books in your classroom to spark children's interest in books.

Story Comprehension

A strong foundation in story comprehension in preschool will help children become good readers in elementary school. Build opportunities for children to make connections between stories and their lives, predict what will happen next in a story, and understand that stories have a beginning, a middle, and an end. Fun after-reading activities, such as storyboard retellings and character interviews, help children deepen their understanding of a story.

Phonological and Phonemic Awareness

Words and their sounds are what children "play with" to build a solid foundation in phonological awareness. Use the activities in *Wild About Literacy* to help children learn listening, rhyming, alliteration, and blending sound skills.

Concepts of Print

It is important for children to learn that print conveys meaning and that there are many great reasons to read and to write. As they watch you read books, children notice that reading is done from top to bottom and from left to right. Song and poem charts, environmental print, and writing activities also help children learn about letters and words, the spaces between words, and the direction in which words are read on a page.

Alphabet Knowledge and Letter Recognition

Name games, word walls, word cards, and alphabet, song, and poem charts help children recognize letters in familiar words and associate the names of letters with their shapes and sounds. Tactile letter shaping, letter sorting, writing, art, and movement activities offer multiple ways for children to learn how to form letters.

Beginning Writing

Children are motivated to learn to write when they discover that what they think and say can be written down and read by others. They learn to write by observing others write. Observing what you write on class charts shows the children that their experiences can be described on charts. Children can also respond to stories by drawing, scribbling, or dictating their stories, thoughts, and ideas.

The activities in *Wild About Literacy* provide guidelines, information, ideas, and activities to teach children skills that will prepare them to become good readers and writers. When introducing a new skill, whether it is singing a new song, identifying a rhyming pattern, or distinguishing letters with straight lines from those with curved lines, use the following instructional sequence to scaffold or support children's learning.

- **Model the skill** by demonstrating how to do it step-by-step. Think aloud so the children can understand your thought process.

- **Invite children to practice** the skill along with you.

- **Encourage children to perform** the skill on their own, providing guidance when needed.

Reading Aloud

Reading books aloud is the foundation of early literacy. Researchers have concluded that reading aloud may be the most important thing we can do to prepare toddlers and preschoolers for learning how to read and to write. *How* you read and what you talk about before and after reading, are just as important as what you read. Consider the following when reading books to young children:

- **Read the book several times** to yourself before sharing it with children. Mark the places at which you would like to pause and ask questions or explain unfamiliar words.
- **Talk about the book cover.** Point out the title, author, and illustrator and talk about what they do. Look at and talk about the art.
- **Create a context.** Share a related personal experience, look at the pictures together, or ask children to predict what might happen in the story.
- **Read slowly** so children can understand and enjoy the rhythm of the words and explore the pictures. Hold the book so everyone can see it.
- **Add drama** to your reading by using different voices and simple props. Don't be afraid to be silly or dramatic!
- **Invite children to join in** on repeating lines and phrases such as, *I'll huff and I'll puff, and I'll blow your house in!*
- **Point to the illustrations** to clarify the meaning of unfamiliar words.
- **Use facial expressions, movements, and gestures** to demonstrate the meaning of action words.

■ **Ask open-ended questions** after reading to help children think about, remember, and discuss the story. Encourage them to connect the story to their life. Remember to pause for at least 10 seconds after asking a question to give the children time to think about their answers.

The Three Rs of Preschool: Rhythm, Rhyme, and Repetition

Rhyming and singing are great fun. They are also wonderful ways for children to hear the rhythms and patterns of language and to play with words and practice their sounds—important steps to learning to read. Rhythm, rhyme, and repetition make words memorable. The songs and poems children learn by heart today will help them learn to read the words in books tomorrow.

■ **Sing a song or recite a poem a few times** before inviting children to join in.

■ **Add movements and gestures** to demonstrate the actions in a song or poem. Invite children to clap or sway to the rhythm.

■ **Identify rhyming words.** As you sing a song or recite a poem, emphasize the rhyming words by chanting or singing them in a softer voice or louder voice.

■ **Print the words to the song or poem** on a chart. You may want to add pictures for key words: *Twinkle, twinkle, little* ★.

The Literacy Scope and Sequence

Although all children develop at their own rate and in their own way, every child needs to develop the following essential literacy skills:

Oral Language: Listening and Understanding	■ Listens to others with understanding ■ Listens attentively to stories, poems, and songs ■ Uses active listening and viewing ■ Recognizes environmental sounds ■ Listens to and follows directions ■ Develops varied and complex vocabulary ■ Listens to music ■ Listens to the sounds produced by musical instruments
Oral Language: Speaking and Communicating	■ Uses language to express actions ■ Identifies common objects and interprets pictures ■ Uses language for conversation and to communicate information, experiences, ideas, thoughts, feelings, opinions, needs, wants, and questions ■ Retells a familiar story ■ Uses language to recall a sequence of events ■ Develops and uses new vocabulary ■ Uses positional words in proper context ■ Speaks in simple sentences
Book Appreciation and Knowledge	■ Listens to and discusses stories (realistic and fantasy) ■ Listens to and discusses nonfiction and concept books ■ Learns how to handle, care for, and turn the pages of a book ■ Selects theme-related books to "read" alone or with other children ■ Draws pictures based on a story ■ Joins in the reading of familiar/predictable/pattern books ■ Seeks information from nonfiction texts
Story Comprehension	■ Understands the literal meaning of a story ■ Predicts an outcome and/or what will happen next in a story ■ Connects information from a story to life experiences ■ Differentiates reality from fantasy ■ Interprets illustrations ■ Develops awareness of cause and effect ■ Uses experiences to understand characters' feeling and motivations ■ Retells or acts out stories in dramatic play ■ Discusses story elements (character, setting, plot) ■ Compares and contrasts characters, settings, and events ■ Understands that stories have a beginning, middle, and end

Phonological and Phonemic Awareness	■ Listens to and identifies sounds in words (phonemes)
	■ Listens to rhyming words
	■ Recognizes rhyming words
	■ Generates rhyming words
	■ Understands that different words begin with the same sound (alliteration)
	■ Distinguishes words in a sentence
	■ Listens to and distinguishes syllables in words by clapping, stomping, or finger tapping
	■ Listens to and begins to notice beginning sounds in words
	■ Begins to notice ending sounds in words
	■ Identifies initial sound in words
	■ Segments, blends, and deletes syllables in compound words
	■ Listens to and begins to blend beginning and ending sounds in words (onset and rime)
	■ Listens to and begins to blend three- and four-phoneme words
	■ Begins to become familiar with onomatopoeia (words that have a sound that imitates or suggests its meaning, such as *quack*, *hiss*, or *woof*)

Concepts of Print	■ Understands that a book has a title, author, and illustrator
	■ Identifies the book author and illustrator
	■ Locates the book title
	■ Understands that English is read from left to right
	■ Understands that English is read from top to bottom
	■ Holds a book correctly (right side up)
	■ Recognizes local environmental print
	■ Understands that print conveys meaning
	■ Recognizes the association between spoken and written words
	■ Recognizes that letters are grouped to form words
	■ Recognizes that words are separated by spaces
	■ Recognizes familiar words
	■ Understands the different functions of forms of print, such as signs, letters, lists, menus, and messages

Alphabet Knowledge and Letter Recognition	■ Begins to recognize letters
	■ Recognizes his or her first name in print
	■ Understands that the alphabet is made up of letters that each have a different name
	■ Distinguishes letter shapes (straight line, curvy line, slanted line, and so on)
	■ Associates names of letters with their shapes
	■ Notices the beginning letters in familiar words
	■ Identifies the first letters in words
	■ Associates names of letters with their sounds

Beginning Writing	■ Experiments with a variety of writing tools and materials
	■ Dictates stories or experiences
	■ Represents stories, ideas, and experiences through scribbles, shapes, drawings
	■ Writes for many purposes (signs, labels, stories, messages)
	■ Attempts to write his or her name

Setting Up the Classroom

Help children develop their literacy skills by including many literacy-focused elements in your classroom. These can include the following:

- **Wall displays** that the children create and that provide opportunites to engage children in discussion by asking them questions about the displays.
- **Classroom charts** that reflect who is in your classroom and what goes on in your classroom. You can use them to organize classroom jobs or to designate who will be classroom buddies. Children can look at and "read" these charts to find out information.
- **Music and sound recordings** that help children learn that language has many sounds.
- **Book and listening corners** that make it possible for individual children to explore books and stories about many topics.

After setting up your classroom during the first few weeks of school, introduce one or two additional ideas each week that relate to the topic you are teaching or the interests of the children. Take down one of the charts, displays, recordings, or corners in your classroom before you replace it with another.

Activities and Charts for the First Few Weeks of School

Set up your classroom with the following charts at the beginning of the school. Keep them up all year long.

- **Job Chart**—Create a class Job or Helper chart. With the children, brainstorm a list of classroom jobs and list them on a large chart. Illustrate each job with a photograph or simple drawing. Rotate children's name cards on the Job chart each week so that everyone gets a chance to try each job. At the beginning of each week, encourage the children to find their name on the chart and figure out which job they have.

- **Class Birthday Chart**—Make a class birthday chart with twelve columns—one for each month of the year. In each column, place a name card and/or photograph of each child who has a birthday in that month.

■ **Buddy Chart**—Have the children learn and play with a designated buddy during center time. When assigning buddies, pair children who are not already good friends. Mix children by gender, culture, learning style, and/or personality. For example, you might pair a shy child with an outgoing one. Make a Buddy chart that shows the names of buddies as paired. Post it at the children's eye level so they can see who their buddy is. Review the chart with the children, and explain that they will be with their buddies while in the centers. Explain that a buddy is a friend, someone you do things with. Buddies share, take turns, and work together.

Teacher Tip: You may want to keep the same buddies together for the week or make new buddy pairs each day. When the children arrive at school, you may want to place matching stickers on each buddy's shirt. Then have the children find their buddy by looking for the matching sticker.

■ **Class Name Chart**—Begin a Class Name chart to use throughout the year to help the children learn letters, letter sounds, and each other's names. Say, *We are going to make a big chart with everyone's name on it. With your help, I am going to write the names in a special order—alphabetical order. It will be just like the order of the letters on our alphabet chart, in the alphabet song, and in alphabet books.* Point to the letter "A" on your alphabet chart and say, *The first letter of the alphabet is the letter "A." If your name starts with the letter "A," raise your hand. Aaron, your name starts with the letter "A." I am going to write your name here under the letter "A" on the name chart.* Write the name as you say each letter aloud—A-A-R-O-N. Ask, *Who else has a name that begins with the letter "A"? Aisha, your name also begins with the letter "A."* Write the second name directly under the first name. Follow this procedure for the next five letters of the alphabet. Add to the name chart each day until it is complete.

■ **"Here We Are Together"**—Print one child's name on an index card. Make one for each child in the class, and then create a duplicate set of cards. You may want to add photos, stickers, stamps, or simple pictures to help the children recognize their names.

Sing the following song with individual children to help them recognize their name and learn the names of the children in the class. Before singing the song, give one child a name card with his name on it. Place two or three name cards on the table. One card should be the child's name. Hold up the other name card with the child's name on it. Ask, *Whose name is this?* Help the child make the match. You may also want to say the letters in the child's name as you point to them on the name card. Tell the child you are going to sing a song that has his name in it. Sing "Here We Are Together" and point to the child as you sing his name. Invite the other children to sing the song with you.

> **Here We Are Together**
> (*Tune: "Have You Ever Seen a Lassie?"*)
> Here we are together, together, together,
> Here we are together, together again.
> Here's *Asante, Asante, Asante, Asante.* (*Insert child's name.*)
> Here we are together, together again.

Wall Displays

- **Reading Wall Display**—Create a wall display with snapshots of the children "reading" books in the classroom. This will help the children see themselves as readers and motivate them to learn the skills they will need to get ready to read.

- **Pictures Tell a Story Wall Display**—Cartoons, art prints, posters, advertisements, picture book covers, and photographs can tell stories without words. Choose a few pictures with people or animals in interesting poses or situations to display in a special place in the room (or feature a different picture each day). Encourage the children to invent stories that explain what is happening in the pictures and/or what is about to happen.

- **Clothing Wall Display**—Create a Clothing wall display with labeled pictures or photos of different types of clothing. Invite the children to look at, name, and describe the articles of clothing. Ask questions such as, *What color is this shirt? What pattern do you see on the necktie?*

- **Food Wall Display**—Cut out pictures from grocery-store flyers to create a Food wall display. You may want to sort the foods into categories—fruits, vegetables, meat and poultry, and so on. Encourage the children to look at the pictures and identify and talk about the different foods.

■ **Feelings Wall Display**—Make a Feelings wall display with labeled photographs of children and grownups showing different emotions in a variety of situations. Ask the children to describe what they see in the photographs. *What is happening in this picture? How do you think the girl on the swing feels? How can you tell?*

■ **Friends-Together Wall Display**—Create a Friends-Together wall display with photographs of friends doing activities together. You can cut out pictures from magazines or take photos of the children in your class playing and working together (building with blocks, painting a picture, eating, helping one another, and so on). Label the pictures: "Friends help each other"; "Friends play together"; and so on. Ask caregivers to bring in pictures of their children and their friends to add to the display. Emphasize that friends can be family members, and pets, too. Encourage children to look at and talk about the photographs.

■ **Solar-System Wall Display**—Create a Solar-System wall display that includes pictures of stars that show constellations such as the Great Bear (including the Big Dipper) and Leo the Lion. Encourage the children to look at and talk about the pictures.

■ **Nighttime Wall Display**—Create a Nighttime wall display of pictures and photographs. Feature outdoor scenes (country and city settings) as well as indoor scenes of parents putting children to bed.

■ **Seasons Wall Display**—Create a chart with four headings, one for each season. Under each heading, display pictures that feature activities associated with the season, such as building snowmen in the winter, splashing in puddles in the spring, swimming in the summer, and picking apples in the fall. Encourage the children to describe what they see in each picture. Ask, *Which season is shown in this picture? Why do you think that?*

Classroom Charts

■ **Question-of-the-Day Chart**—At the top of a large sheet of chart paper, write the question: *Do you like rice?* Then draw a vertical line down the middle of the paper to create two columns. Label the left column *YES* and the right column *NO*. Display the chart on an easel or on a wall at the children's eye level and place markers nearby. As the children arrive and settle down, direct them and their parents or caregivers to the chart. Encourage parents and caregivers to read the question to their child. Have the children answer the question and write their names in the *YES* or *NO* columns. Change the question each day. Here are some possibilities:

- Do you like bananas?
- Have you ever eaten a tamale?
- Do you like to help cook?
- Do you like to drink apple juice?
- Did you wear a coat today?
- Do you have any letters on your clothes?
- Do your shoes have laces?
- Did you dress yourself today?

Mirror Chart—Hang a mirror at the children's eye level. Around the mirror, display small photographs or pictures of faces expressing a wide range of emotions. Encourage the children to look at themselves in the mirror and make faces that show different emotions. Ask, *How does your face look when you feel surprised? When you feel mad?*

How Do You Feel Today? Chart—On a large sheet of chart paper, write the question, *How do you feel today?* Make three columns. In the first column, draw a happy face and write the word *happy* underneath. In the second column, draw and label a sad face. In the third column, draw and label a silly face. Display the chart on an easel or on a wall at the children's eye level and place markers and/or children's name cards nearby. As the children arrive in the morning, direct them and their parents or caregivers to the chart. Encourage parents and caregivers to read the question to their children. Have the children write their names or place their name cards in the column that shows how they feel. Occasionally change the third face and face label to reflect other feelings such as shy, frustrated, angry, or excited.

Music and Sound Recordings

Musical Recordings—Bring in a diverse collection of music—children's music, classical, jazz, rock, reggae, folk, country, and so on. Play instrumental music as children draw, paint, eat, or rest. Schedule frequent "Move to the Music" breaks and join the children in dancing, clapping, twirling scarves, or swaying to the sounds. Talk about the music—is it fast or slow? Loud or quiet? Ask, *How does the music make you feel? Which type of music do you like best?*

■ **Sounds All Around**—Create a tape recording of familiar sounds in the environment, such as a dog barking, a car horn honking, a door closing, a clock ticking, and so on. Play the tape and invite the children to name the sounds they hear.

Book and Listening Corners

■ **Book-Browsing Boxes**—Set up a classroom library the children can use independently. Create book-browsing boxes of plastic bins or cardboard boxes. Fill each book-browsing box with books that focus on one topic, such as feelings, families, nighttime, or animals. Label each box with words and a matching picture or symbol so the children can identify the contents on their own. Include both fiction and nonfiction books. Place three or four books into each box and add to the boxes throughout the year. At any one time, your classroom library should have one or two boxes that relate to the topic you are teaching. Rotate the other book-browsing boxes in the classroom library throughout the year.

■ **Listening Corner**—Create a listening corner in the Pretend and Play Center with storytelling CDs and tape recordings. Borrow them from your local library or create homemade recordings of yourself and the children telling stories.

Setting Up the Classroom— Checklist

The way you arrange your physical space greatly influences how children play, work, and learn. Following is a checklist to help you create an environment that supports children as they learn about language and the world of print and books.

- Is children's work displayed at their eye level around the room?

- Are children's names written in different places around the room? (on cubbies, helper chart, and so on)

- Is environmental print displayed at children's eye level?

- Is there an alphabet chart displayed at children's eye level?

- Are topic-related posters and wall displays placed where children can easily see and talk about the pictures?

- Are art supplies and other materials labeled?

- Are chairs and other furniture arranged so children can talk and play together?

- Is the classroom space divided into small learning centers?

- Is each learning center labeled with words and/or pictures that children can understand?

- Is there a variety of writing tools (paper, pencils, markers, crayons, and so on) in each learning center?

- Are there theme-related books in the learning centers?

- Are books in the Library Center easy for children to see and to reach?

- Is there a variety of fiction and nonfiction books in the Library Center? Are there books that reflect children's racial and ethnic backgrounds, as well as books from diverse cultures?

- Is there a CD or tape player? Are there different types of musical recordings for children to listen and move to during the day?

Glossary

alliteration: repeating the same sound at the beginning of words, as in *Sally sells seashells by the seashore*

alphabet knowledge: being able to name and write the 26 letters of the alphabet

blending: putting together individual sounds to make words (*I'm thinking of a word that names an animal. It has these sounds: /p/ /i/ /g/. What's the word?*)

characters: the people or animals in a story

concepts of print: children's understanding of the different ways we use written language—as in letters, recipes, labels, and stories—as well as the way we write and read print. For example, printed words are separated by spaces; we read from left to right and from top to bottom.

environmental print: the written letters and words we see every day in our homes and neighborhoods that we recognize from the pictures, colors, and shapes that surround them. Examples include food and clothing labels, store logos, and road signs.

fiction: stories, essays, articles, and books that tell a made-up story, such as storybooks, fairy tales, and folktales

literacy: the skills and activities involved in speaking, listening, reading, and writing

making predictions: using information that you already know to guess what a story will be about or what will happen next

modeling: showing children how to do a task or skill before asking them to do it on their own

nonfiction: stories, essays, articles, and books that provide information or facts about a subject, including biographies and concept books (books about colors, shapes, sizes, and so on)

onset and rime: Onset is the initial consonant sound(s) in a syllable; rime is the part that contains the vowel and all that follows it. In the word *cat*, /c/ is the onset and /at/ is the rime. In the word *bat*, /b/ is the onset and /at/ is the rime.

open-ended questions: questions that can't be answered with a yes or no answer. For example: *What part of the story did you like best?*

phonemic awareness: the ability to hear and identify the individual sounds in *spoken* words. When the children hear the individual /m/, /o/, and /p/ sounds that make up the word *mop*, they are developing phonemic awareness. [In *Wild About Literacy*, the *letter* is written in quotation marks ("d"), while the *sound of the letter* is written between two slashes (/d/).]

phonics: a skill that matches *written* letters and words with the sounds they make. A child who looks at the printed word *dog* and sounds it out is using phonics. Children need a solid foundation in phonological awareness before they learn phonics.

phonological awareness: a broad range of listening skills—from being able to hear and recognize sounds in the environment to paying attention to and manipulating the individual sounds in words. Rhyming, singing, and clapping the syllables in words are examples of activities that build phonological awareness.

picture walk: turning the pages of a book from the beginning to end and asking children to look at and talk about the illustrations. Picture walks before reading help prepare children for listening. Picture walks after reading help children retell the story.

plot: what happens in the beginning, middle, and end of a story

print-rich environment: a classroom that displays words and letters that are meaningful to children in places in which children can see and interact with them

retell: to tell a story in your own words and in the correct order or sequence

rhyme: the repetition of the ending sound of a word, as in Jack and *Jill* went up the *hill*

scaffolding: helping children learn a new skill step-by-step and gradually removing support as children become able to perform the skill on their own

segmenting: taking spoken words apart sound by sound. Clapping the parts or syllables in words and names is an example of segmenting (*A-bi-yo-yo*; *Ben-ja-min*; and so on).

setting: where and when a story takes place

shared reading: when a teacher reads aloud a Big Book or chart with large print and encourages children to read along on parts they can remember or guess

shared writing: when children dictate their stories or ideas for the teacher to write

spoken or oral language: the language we use to talk and listen

story structure: the way stories are organized into a beginning, a middle, and an end

syllable: a word part that contains a vowel sound. The word *dog* has one syllable. The word *an-i-mal* has three syllables.

vocabulary: knowing the meaning of the words we use when we speak, listen, read, and write

word play: playing with the beginning, middle, and ending sounds of words for fun and to learn how words work

Chapter 1

Learning Center Activities

Depending on the children's interests, you may want to modify existing centers and add new centers. When appropriate, demonstrate and model the activities. Invite the children to explore the materials in the centers and the activities on their own and in small groups. Encourage them to interact with one another and collaborate in their play. Provide assistance as needed. As you talk to the children about what they are doing, use the suggested vocabulary words in ways that help the children understand their meaning.

The activities in this chapter are grouped alphabetically by topic and then by age (3+ or 4+) within each topic or theme, and have the following components:

Skill Focus	**Materials**
Theme Connection(s)	**Preparation (if necessary)**
Vocabulary	**What to Do**

Skill Focus—lists the literacy skills that the activity addresses and other skills that young children need to learn, such as fine motor skills or emotional awareness.

Theme Connections—lists one or two familiar early childhood themes that the activity covers.

Vocabulary—lists words that are part of the activity. Use these when you are engaging children in the activity, defining their meaning if necessary. Repeat these words throughout the day so children hear the words used in context and can begin to understand how each word is used.

Materials—lists, in alphabetical order, the materials you will need to do the activity. Be sure you have the materials you need before you begin the activity.

Preparation—If the activity needs any preparation, such as writing a song or poem on chart paper or preparing a chart, what you need to do is described in this section.

What to Do—Step by step, this section outlines how to engage children in the activity.

In addition, some activities include ideas that build on the main activity or extend it to another curriculum area.

A Note About Repetition: You will find the same songs, poems, and books used in multiple activities in *Wild About Literacy*. Children benefit and learn from repetition. When children hear a familiar song or poem, they may learn something new or solidify what they already know. Using a familiar song or story to teach a new skill is a technique used by many teachers, which is why you will find repetition in this book.

Library Center—Book-Browsing Boxes

Skill Focus
Book Care and Handling
Choosing Books
Concepts of Print

Theme Connection
All About Me

Vocabulary

author	picture
back cover	read
front cover	return
illustration	rules
illustrator	title
label	

Materials

fiction and nonfiction books on different topics and genres

magazines or catalogs

markers or crayons

paper

scissors

tape or glue

Click on the
Between the Lions website!
pbskids.org/lions/gryphonhouse

Books featured on
Between the Lions
Recommended Books
Song: Read a Book Today!

Preparation

☐ Set up book-browsing boxes with many different kinds of books.

☐ Create a written label for each book-browsing box.

☐ Draw a picture (or cut out a picture from a magazine or catalog) that relates to each book-browsing book topic, and put this next to the written label, so the children know the kind of books that are in each box.

☐ Rotate the boxes into the Library Center throughout the year. Place one or two boxes in the center. Replace a box when you begin a new topic or when the children express interest in a topic.

What to Do

☐ Explain to the children that the pictures on the labels of the book-browsing boxes will help them select the kind of book they want to read and will also help them put the book away.

☐ Ask, *If you want a fairy-tale book, which box would you look in? This box has a magic wand on the label, so this is the box with the fairy tales, such as Cinderella. When you are finished reading the fairy tale, where will you put it? Look, here is an alphabet book we read last week. Can you help me find which box to put it in?* (The box decorated with the alphabet letters.)

☐ Encourage the children to select books that interest them and to look at the words and pictures on their own or with another child.

☐ Model how to look at the illustration on a book cover, predict what the book will be about, and decide whether you want to read it. Go over basic library rules about how to handle and care for books.

Skill Focus
Book Care and Handling
Choosing Books
Concepts of Print

Theme Connection
All About Me

Library Center—Choosing Interesting Books

What to Do

- Encourage the children to select books that interest them and to look at the words and pictures on their own or with another child.
- Model how to look at the illustration on a book cover, predict what the book will be about, and decide whether you want to read it. *Look, this book has a picture of a girl holding a baby on the cover. I think she's holding her baby sister. Don't you have a baby sister, Priscilla? You might like to read this book.*
- Demonstrate how to hold, handle, and care for a book.
- Show the children where to begin reading and how to turn the pages. Read parts of the book aloud and talk to the children about the book. *What do you see on this page? What do you think is happening? I see that you have picked another book by Irene Smalls. This one is called* Kevin and His Dad. *Let's look at the pictures and see what Kevin and his dad do together.*
- Include in your classroom library a variety of fiction and nonfiction books about different kinds of families, including those that reflect the families of the children in your class.

Extension Idea

Suggest that the children draw a picture or write or dictate a story about one of the books.

Vocabulary

author	handle
back cover	illustration
care for	illustrator
cover	page
family	predict
front cover	title

Materials

fiction and nonfiction books about families or another topic

Click on the *Between the Lions* website!
pbskids.org/lions/gryphonhouse

Song: Read a Book Today!

ABC Center—Alphabet Sponges

AGE 3+

Skill Focus
Letter Recognition
Name Recognition

Theme Connections
All About Me
Alphabet

Vocabulary

alphabet   name
letter   sponges
match   word

Materials

alphabet chart, alphabet book
   (optional)
alphabet sponges
paint
paper
scissors

Preparation

☒ Cut out squares of paper.
☒ Arrange cut-out squares of paper, alphabet sponges, and paint on a table.

What to Do

☒ Show the children how to press an alphabet sponge into the paint and then onto the paper to make a letter. The children can choose letters randomly, or you can preselect letter sponges that correspond to the letters in their first name.

☒ Talk to the children about their letters. Help them match their letters to the letters in their name, to an alphabet chart, to an alphabet book, or to words that are posted in your classroom.

Extension Idea

Show the children alphabet books such as *The Farm Alphabet Book* by Jane Miller or *Eating the Alphabet* by Lois Ehlert and then suggest that the children use the alphabet sponges to make alphabet pictures by stamping one letter on a piece of paper and then making a drawing of something that begins with that letter on the paper. Leave the alphabet books out for the children to use as they create their alphabet pictures.

Click on the *Between the Lions* website!
pbskids.org/lions/gryphonhouse

Song: Library A to Z
Game: ABCD Watermelon

Skill Focus
Letter Recognition

Theme Connections
All About Me
Alphabet
Shapes

ABC Center— Letter Match

AGE 3+

Preparation

◻ Make a name card for each child by writing each name on an index card, using uppercase letters for the first letter and lowercase letters for the remaining letters.

What to Do

◻ On a table, arrange the name cards and plastic uppercase letters that correspond to the first letters in the children's first names.

◻ The children hunt for the plastic letter that matches the first letter on their name card.

◻ Suggest that the children trace the plastic letter with their fingers as they say the name of the letter and describe how the letter looks. Ask, *Does it have straight lines, slanted lines, curvy lines, circles?*

Extension Idea

Have the children repeat aloud the first letter in their name. Tell the children the sound that the letter makes. Say, *Sam, your name begins with the letter "S." The letter "S" makes the /s/ sound. Let's say it together—/s/. Sandy and Simone have names that also begin with the /s/ sound!*

Vocabulary

circle	match
curvy	slanted
first name	straight
letter	trace

Materials

blank index cards

markers

plastic uppercase letters

Click on the *Between the Lions* website!

pbskids.org/lions/gryphonhouse

Song: Upper and Lowercase

ABC Center— Letter Shaping

Skill Focus
Fine Motor Skills
Letter Formation
Letter Recognition

Theme Connections
Alphabet
Shapes

Vocabulary

clay
roll

shape
straight line

Materials

alphabet chart
blank index cards
markers
modeling clay
pipe cleaners
plastic straws cut into long and
    short pieces

Preparation
🔲 Write the uppercase and lowercase "Ll" on an index card to create a letter "Ll" card.

What to Do

🔲 Select one letter of the alphabet. Focus on a letter that relates to a classroom topic, a book you are reading to the children, or something that is happening in the classroom or is important to the children. In this case, the letter "Ll" is the example.

🔲 Display the letter "Ll" card. Use your finger to trace over both the lowercase and uppercase letter "Ll" on the card to show the children how to form the letter.

🔲 Show the children how to shape pipe cleaners or to roll "snakes" of clay with the palms of their hands and form the letter "Ll."

🔲 Have the children use plastic straw pieces to form the letter "L."

Extension Idea

Repeat with the other letters of the alphabet until the children have explored the uppercase and lowercase shapes of all of the letters of the alphabet.

Click on the *Between the Lions* website!
pbskids.org/lions/gryphonhouse

Song: Upper and Lowercase
Game: Monkey Match (upper and lowercase)

Skill Focus

Creative Expression
Fine Motor Skills
Letter Recognition
Vocabulary

Theme Connections

Alphabet
Shapes

ABC Center—Decorate Letter "Bb"

AGE 3+

Preparation

- Draw very large outlines of uppercase "B" and lowercase "b" on multiple sheets of paper.
- Cut enough for each child to have one uppercase letter "B" and one lowercase letter "b."

What to Do

- Provide an uppercase "B" and lowercase "b" on paper for every child.
- Encourage the children to explore the shape of the letters by tracing the outlines of the letters with their fingers.
- Have the children use blue markers and crayons to decorate the letters with polka dots, stripes, squiggles, zigzags, and curly and wiggly lines.
- Encourage them to talk about and describe the decorative marks they are making.

Note: Throughout the year, use this approach with other letters, focusing on letters that relate to poems or stories you are reading to the children, or to your classroom topic.

Extension Idea

Use masking tape to make an uppercase "B" and lowercase "b" on the floor. Encourage the children to walk along the outlines of the letters.

Vocabulary

blue
curly
lines
polka dots

stripes
wiggly
zigzags

Materials

blue crayons and markers
scissors
white paper

Click on the *Between the Lions* website!
pbskids.org/lions/gryphonhouse

Games:
- Monkey Match (upper and lowercase)
- Sky Riding

ABC Center— Letter Sort

Skill Focus

Compare and Contrast
Letter Recognition
Vocabulary

Theme Connections

Alphabet
Shapes

Vocabulary

circle	slanted
curvy	sort
letter	straight
shape	

Materials

bag
marker
paper
plastic uppercase letters

Preparation

☒ Place plastic letters "F," "H," "T," "C," "S," "O" into a bag. Divide a piece of paper in half by drawing a line down the middle. Draw a straight line at the top of the left side and a curvy line at the top of the right side.

What to Do

☒ Engage the children in a discussion about the shapes of letters. Suggest that one way letters can be sorted is by whether they have straight or curvy lines.

☒ Explain that if the letter has straight lines it belongs on the side with the straight line. If the letter has curvy lines, it belongs on the side with the curvy line.

☒ Have the children take one letter out of the bag at a time, look at it and decide where to place it on the paper.

☒ Think aloud as you model the activity for the children. Say, *Let's take a good look at the letter "T." Move your finger along the lines. Are the lines curvy? Are they straight? I see a straight line here and another there. The letter "T" has two straight lines. So it goes on this side of the paper with the straight line.*

Extension Idea

On another day, continue with more letters of the alphabet. When appropriate, add letters that are both straight and curvy such as "B," "P," and "D." Before adding these letters, create a chart that has three columns, one for letters that have only straight lines, one for letters that have only curvy lines, and one for letters that have both curvy and straight lines.

Click on the *Between the Lions* website!
pbskids.org/lions/gryphonhouse

Games

☒ ABCD Watermelon
☒ Sky Riding

Skill Focus

Compare and Contrast
Fine Motor Skills
Letter Recognition

Theme Connections

Alphabet
Shapes

ABC Center—Uppercase and Lowercase Letter Sort

Preparation

☒ Use blank index cards and markers to create letter cards, one for each letter. Write both the uppercase and lowercase letters on each card.

☒ Place all the magnetic letters in a box.

What to Do

☒ Point to one letter card. This activity uses the letter "Ll" card.

☒ Say, *This card shows a big (uppercase) "L" and a little (lowercase) "l." In this box, there are some uppercase or big letters. We're going to find all the uppercase "L" letters and put them here on the left side of the cookie sheet. We'll put all the other letters here on the right side of the cookie sheet.*

☒ Have the children sort the letters with you. As you take the letters out of the box, comment on their shapes. Say, *This letter has two straight lines, just like the big "L" on the letter "L" card. It's an "L"! Let's put it here on the left side. This letter has curvy lines. It doesn't look like an "L." Where should we put it?*

☒ When you've sorted the letters, encourage volunteers to identify the letters by name.

☒ On another day, repeat the process as you search the lowercase letter box for the letter "l."

Extension Idea

With masking tape or chalk, make a large uppercase letter "L" and a large lowercase letter "l" side by side on the ground. Have the children line up and, one by one, take big steps as they march along the uppercase letter "L" from top to bottom. Have them take little steps along the lowercase letter "l." As they march, have the children clap or chant the letter name. Repeat with other letters of the alphabet.

Vocabulary

big	lowercase
curvy	match
find	straight line
letter	uppercase
little	

Materials

blank index cards

cookie sheet

magnetic letters ("Ll," "Ss," "Uu," and "Mm")

markers

two boxes (one for uppercase letters and one for lowercase letters)

Click on the *Between the Lions* website!

pbskids.org/lions/gryphonhouse

Song: Upper and Lowercase
Games:

☒ Monkey Match (upper and lowercase)

☒ Sky Riding

AGE 3+

ABC Center— Letter Search ("Cc," "Rr," "Ss")

Vocabulary

big	search
find	small
letter	uppercase
lowercase	

Materials

advertisement flyers
glue sticks
magazines
newspapers
scissors
three pieces of poster paper, each with a letter heading: "Cc," "Rr," or "Ss"

Preparation

◼ Prepare three pieces of poster paper. Write either "Cc," "Rr," or "Ss" at the top.

What to Do

◼ Show the children the three pieces of poster paper, each with a letter heading: "Cc," "Rr," or "Ss."
◼ Have the children search through flyers, magazines, and newspapers and cut out the uppercase and lowercase letters "Cc," "Rr," and "Ss" that they find.
◼ Help them paste the letters on the appropriate poster. Look at and talk about the completed posters together.

Extension Idea

Use the same approach for other letters of the alphabet.

Click on the *Between the Lions* website!
pbskids.org/lions/gryphonhouse

Song: Library A to Z
Game: Sky Riding

Skill Focus
Letter Recognition
Name Recognition

Theme Connections
Alphabet
Shapes

ABC Center— More Letter Matching

AGE
4+

Preparation

◻ Use blank index cards and markers to make a name card for each child. (The letters on the name card should be the same dimensions as the plastic letters you use.)

What to Do

◻ Prepare a container for each child with his name card and plastic letters that correspond to his first name.

◻ The children place their name cards in front of them and match the plastic letters to the letters on their name cards in the correct order.

◻ If necessary, model the process. Point to a child's name card. Say, *Your name is Lonnie. Let's say the letters in your name:* L-O-N-N-I-E. *This is the letter "L." It's the first letter in your name. Let's find the letter "L." It has all straight lines. Here it is. Can you place it under the letter "L" on your name card? The next letter looks like this. It is an "O." It is shaped like a circle.*

◻ Continue to model the process going from left to right.

Extension Idea

Hide the children's name cards in the classroom. Challenge the children to find their name cards.

Vocabulary

first	name
last	next
letter	same
match	

Materials

blank index cards
markers
plastic letters
small containers

Click on the
*Between the
Lions* website!
pbskids.org/lions/gryphonhouse

Games:
◻ ABCD Watermelon
◻ Monkey Match (upper and lowercase)

ABC Center—Fish for "c-a-n"

Skill Focus
Fine Motor Skills
Letter Recognition
Vocabulary
Word Recognition

Theme Connection
Alphabet

Vocabulary

first	middle
last	second
letter	third
magnet	word
match	

Materials

blank index card

bucket or bin

magnet

markers

ruler

several sets of magnetic letters:
  "c," "a," and "n"

string

Preparation

- Write *can* on an index card to create a *can* word card.
- Tie a magnet to one end of a string and tie the other end to a ruler to make a magnetic fishing pole.
- Place the letters in a bucket or bin.

What to Do

- Display the *can* word card.
- Have the children repeat the word with you and identify the first letter: "c."
- Suggest that the children fish for the letters in *can*, then arrange the letters to match the letters on the word card.

Extension Idea

Suggest that the children fish for the letters in their names.

Listening and Talking Together

This chapter of *Wild About Literacy* focuses on listening and talking with children, which is one of the building blocks of early literacy (see The Literacy Scope and Sequence on pages 14–15). Before children become readers, they need to listen and talk a lot. The activities that follow will help you create a classroom that is alive with the sounds of children talking, singing, and playing with the sounds in words. Fill the days with conversation about what the children are doing and the books you are reading, and introduce new words and concepts as you invite children to talk about their lives.

The activities in this chapter are grouped alphabetically by topic and then by age (3+ or 4+) within each topic or theme. The activities have the following components:

Skill Focus	**Materials**
Theme Connection(s)	**Preparation (if necessary)**
Vocabulary	**What to Do**

Skill Focus—lists the literacy skills that the activity addresses and other skills that young children need to learn, such as fine motor skills or emotional awareness.

Theme Connections—lists one or two familiar early childhood themes that the activity covers. If more than one theme is listed, the first is the one with the strongest connection.

Vocabulary—lists words that are part of the activity. Use these when you are engaging children in the activity, defining their meaning if necessary. Repeat these words throughout the day so children hear the words used in context and can begin to understand how each word is used.

Materials—lists, in alphabetical order, the materials you will need to do the activity. Be sure you have the materials you need before you begin the activity.

A Note About Repetition: You will find the same songs, poems, and books used in multiple activities in *Wild About Literacy*. Children benefit and learn from repetition. When children hear a familiar song or poem, they may learn something new or solidify what they already know. Using a familiar song or story to teach a new skill is a technique used by many teachers, which is why you will find repetition in this book.

Preparation—If the activity needs any preparation, such as writing a song or poem on chart paper or preparing a chart, what you need to do is described in this section.

What to Do—Step by step, this section outlines how to engage children in the activity.

In addition, many activities include ideas that build on the main activity, extend it to another curriculum area, or suggest books that relate to the activity.

The following children's books are used in one or more activities in this chapter:

The Lion and the Mouse by Bernadette Watts (see page 49)
The Way I Feel by Janan Cain (see page 42)

In addition, many children's books are suggested as a way to extend an activity. Some of the book suggestions include:

Animals in Winter by Henrietta Bancroft and Helen K. Davie
Bedtime for Little Bears! by David Bedford and Caroline Pedler
Charlie Parker Played Be Bop by Chris Raschka [featured on a *Between the Lions* episode]
Come On, Rain! by Karen Hesse and Jon J. Muth
Grandfather Twilight by Barbara Helen Berger
Grandma Lena's Big Ol' Turnip by Denia Lewis Hester
Ruby Sings the Blues by Niki Daly [featured on a *Between the Lions* episode]
Sleep, Black Bear, Sleep by Jane Yolen, Heidi Y. Stemple, and Brooke Dyer
Sleepy Bears by Mem Fox and Kerry Argent
Sounds All Around by Wendy Pfeffer and Holly Keller
Thirteen Moons on Turtle's Back: A Native American Year of Moons by Joseph Bruchac and Jonathan London
When Sophie Gets Angry—Really, Really Angry by Molly Bang

Click on the *Between the Lions* website! pbskids.org/lions/gryphonhouse

Books featured on *Between the Lions*

Skill Focus
Color Recognition
Following Directions

Theme Connection
Colors

"If You're Wearing Something Blue"

What to Do

◻ Sing "If You're Wearing Something Blue." Ask the children wearing the color named to stand up.

If You're Wearing Something Blue
(*Tune: "Mary Had a Little Lamb"*)
If you're wearing something blue,
Something blue, something blue.
If you're wearing something blue,
Then will you please stand up.

Additional verses:
In place of blue, substitute other color words.

◻ When all the children are standing, change the last line to "Then will you please sit down."

Last verse:
If you're wearing something blue,
Something blue, something blue.
If you're wearing something blue,
Then will you please sit down.

Cleo and Theo's Book Suggestions

My Colors, My World/Mis Colores, Mi Mundo
by Maya Christina Gonzalez
A girl living in the desert describes the colors that remind her of the people and places she loves.

Red Is a Dragon: A Book of Colors
by Roseanne Thong and Grace Lin
The colors that surround a young Chinese American girl remind her of the things that she loves.

Vocabulary

blue	stand up
color	wear
sit down	

Materials

none needed

Click on the *Between the Lions* website!
pbskids.org/lions/gryphonhouse

Story: Spicy Hot Colors
Video Clip: Colorful Foods

All Kinds of Families

Skill Focus
Compare and Contrast
Listening and Speaking
Vocabulary

Theme Connections
Families

Vocabulary

aunt	mother
brother	names
cousin	poster
daughter	same
different	sister
family	son
father	talk
grandfather	uncle
grandmother	

Materials

glue or tape

markers

photographs of each child's family

poster board

Click on the *Between the Lions* website!
pbskids.org/lions/gryphonhouse

Stories:

⊡ My Dog Is as Smelly as Dirty Socks

⊡ Oh, Yes, It Can!

What to Do

⊡ Help each child create a family poster for her family.

⊡ Help the children make name labels for the members of their families.

⊡ Ask questions to help the children observe and talk about the ways their families are the same and different. Ask, *How are families the same? How are they different?*

Extension Idea

Tell the children that *storytellers* are people who tell stories they know by heart. It's fun to listen to storytellers because they are really good at making stories come alive with their hands, voices, and props. Tell the children about a storyteller in your family. Say, *When I was a kid, I loved to visit my grandmother. She would tell us stories about things my mother did when she was a little girl. Those were the stories I liked best.* Ask the children, *Who tells stories in your family?*

Skill Focus

Listening and Speaking
Vocabulary

Theme Connections

Families
Helping

Family Helpers

What to Do

- Talk with the children about how people in your family help one another. Say, *In my family, everyone helps out. My son helps wash the dishes. My daughter helps take out the garbage.*
- Ask, *What do you do to help your family?* Encourage a variety of responses (for example, sort the socks, put away toys, play with the baby).
- Ask questions to prompt the children to think about how they can help out at home. For example, *What can you do to help when your mom or dad is making breakfast or dinner?*

Extension Idea

Create a chart of the things the children do to help out at home. What do most of the children do to help out at home? Are there things that only one child does to help? How do the children help in the classroom? Are they the same as what they do at home?

Vocabulary

baby	help
brother	home
daughter	mother
families	sister
family	son
father	

Materials

none needed

Click on the
*Between the
Lions* website!
pbskids.org/lions/gryphonhouse

Story: Just What Mama Needs

Feelings

Skill Focus
Emotional Awareness
Interpreting Illustrations
Listening and Speaking
Vocabulary

Theme Connection
Feelings

Vocabulary

angry	happy
disappointed	laugh
emotion	sad
feeling	shout
frustrated	stomp

Materials

Feelings wall display
  (see page 19)
The Way I Feel by Janan Cain

Click on the
*Between the
Lions* website!
pbskids.org/lions/gryphonhouse

Stories:
- ◙ Worm Watches
- ◙ Yesterday I Had the Blues

What to Do

◙ Smile and tell the children that you feel happy today because you are so glad to see them.

Feeling Happy

◙ Ask, *Why do you feel happy today?* Encourage a wide variety of responses.

◙ Tell the children that *happy* is a *feeling* or *emotion*. When we are happy, we smile and laugh and feel good inside. Say, *No one feels happy all the time. We have many different kinds of emotions.*

◙ Refer to the Feelings wall display (see page 19). Choose two or three photographs that show different emotions. As you point to each photo, ask, *How do you think the person in this photo feels? How can you tell?*

Feeling Disappointed

◙ If the children are interested in continuing to talk about feelings, show them the Disappointed page in *The Way I Feel*. (If the children are not interested in talking about feelings, continue this conversation later in the day or another day.) Ask, *What is happening in this picture? How do you think the girl feels? Why?* Read aloud the text. Then say, *The girl feels* disappointed *because her friend was going to visit and play with her, but now the friend can't.*

◙ Ask, *What do you think they were going to play?* (They were going to have a tea party!) Emphasize that when we feel disappointed we often feel sad and angry, too. Say, *We can have more than one feeling at a time.*

◙ Tell the children about a time when you felt disappointed. Then ask, *Can you tell about a time when you felt disappointed?*

Feeling Frustrated

- If the children are interested in continuing to talk about feelings, show them the Frustrated page in *The Way I Feel*. (If the children are not interested in talking about feelings, continue this conversation later in the day or another day.) Ask, *What is happening in this picture? How do you think the girl feels? Why?* Read aloud the text. Then say, *The girl feels* frustrated *because she is trying very hard to do something and can't do it.* Ask, *What do you think she is trying to do?* (tie her shoes) Say, *The girl doesn't know whether to keep trying or to give up.*
- Ask, *What do you think? Should she give up or keep trying?*
- Ask the children if they have ever felt frustrated like the girl in the book. *When did you feel frustrated? What did you do? Did you keep trying? Did you give up? Did you ask for help? Did you also feel sad or angry?*

Feeling Angry

- If the children are interested in continuing to talk about feelings, show them the Angry page in *The Way I Feel*. (If the children are not interested in talking about feelings, continue this conversation later in the day or another day.) Ask, *How do you think the girl in this picture feels? How can you tell? Why?* Read aloud the text. Say, *The little girl in the book is so angry she shouts and stomps her feet on the floor.*
- Ask, *Have you ever felt angry? When? What do you do when you feel angry?*

Feeling Thankful

- If the children are interested in continuing to talk about feelings, show them the Thankful page in *The Way I Feel*. (If the children are not interested in talking about feelings, continue this conversation later in the day or another day.) Ask, *How do you think the boy in this picture feels?* Read aloud the text.
- Ask, *Why does the boy feel thankful? How do you feel when someone helps you?* Share with the children some things you feel thankful for. Then ask, *What do you feel thankful for?*

Cleo and Theo's Book Suggestions

Feelings by Shelley Rotner
Color photographs of children and simple text introduce a range of emotions.

Today I Feel Silly & Other Moods That Make My Day
by Jamie Lee Curtis
Young readers identify and explore their many emotions as they read about a young girl whose mood changes from silly to angry to excited.

When Sophie Gets Angry— Really, Really Angry
by Molly Bang
Sophie becomes furious when her mother tells her it's her sister's turn to play with her favorite stuffed gorilla. After some time away, Sophie is able to calm herself down.

Yesterday I Had the Blues
by Jeron Ashford Frame
A young boy uses colors to capture a range of emotions, from "down in my shoes blues" to the kind of greens that "make you want to be Somebody." [featured on a *Between the Lions* episode]

Eating Utensils

Skill Focus
Appreciating Diversity
Listening and Speaking
Vocabulary

Theme Connection
Food

Vocabulary

chops	knife
chopsticks	rice
eat	soup
flip	spatula
fork	spoon

Materials

eating utensils, including a plastic fork, spoon, knife, and a pair of chopsticks

What to Do

- Display eating utensils, including a plastic fork, spoon, knife, and a pair of chopsticks. Hold up each item and ask the children to name them.
- Ask, *What do you use to eat? What do you use to eat soup?* (a spoon) *What do you use to eat rice?* (a fork or chopsticks) *What do people use to cut food into small pieces?* (a knife) *Do you ever use your hands to eat food? What kind of food do you eat with your fingers?* (pizza, fruit, and so on)
- Tell the children that some families use chopsticks to eat certain food. Say, Chopsticks *are a pair of thin sticks that people use to cook and eat with in Korea, China, and other countries. Some families in the United States also eat with chopsticks.*
- Engage the children in a discussion about the utensils they use to eat.

Extension Idea

Show the children how to hold chopsticks. Place the lower chopstick in the base of your thumb and index finger and rest its lower end on your ring finger. Hold the upper chopstick between the tips of your index and middle fingers. Use the tip of your thumb to keep it in place. Demonstrate how to use chopsticks to pick up several small items by moving the upper chopstick with your middle and index fingers. You may want to pass around the chopsticks for the children to try.

Click on the
*Between the
Lions* website!
pbskids.org/lions/gryphonhouse

Story: Bee-bim Bop!

Skill Focus
Listening and Speaking
Vocabulary

Theme Connection
Friends

"Will You Meet a Friend of Mine?"

What to Do

- Talk with the children about being a friend.
- Ask, *What is a friend?* Have them brainstorm a list of words to complete the sentence: A friend is _____.
- Record the children's responses on chart paper.
- Affirm that a friend is someone we like to have fun and play with.
- Display the Buddy chart (see Setting Up the Room, page 17) and tell the children that they will be playing and learning with buddies. Explain that a buddy is a friend. Have buddies find one another and shake hands.

Extension Idea

Form a circle with the children, and teach them "Will You Meet a Friend of Mine?" Then sing it with them. When you sing the last line, signal the child to your left to take a step into the circle. Sing her name: *This is my friend (Zinnia).* Then have the rest of the children wave and say, *Hi, (Zinnia)!*

Will You Meet a Friend of Mine?
(*Tune: "Mary Had a Little Lamb"*)
Will you meet a friend of mine,
Friend of mine, friend of mine?
Will you meet a friend of mine?
This is my friend (child's name). (*Children wave to child.*)

Continue around the circle until you have sung a verse for each child. Invite the children to sing along with you.

Vocabulary

buddy   help
find   play with
friend   shake hands
fun

Materials

chart paper
markers

Friendly Words

Skill Focus
Listening and Speaking
Social and Emotional Awareness
Vocabulary

Theme Connections
Friends
Opposites

Vocabulary

friend	nice
friendly	sad
help	unfriendly
hurt	

Materials

markers
sentence pocket chart
sentence strips

What to Do

▣ Talk with the children about friendly and unfriendly words. Explain that friendly words are nice words that make people feel happy. Unfriendly words can hurt people and make them feel sad.

▣ Give examples of unfriendly words or phrases: "I don't like you," "You can't play," and so on.

▣ Ask, *What are some friendly words? What words do you like to hear your friends say?*

▣ Write the children's responses on sentence strips and display them in a pocket chart. Examples might include:

Hello! How are you?
I like you.
Do you want to play with me?
Can I help you?

Extension Idea

Sing "Friendly Words" with the children.

Friendly Words
(*Tune: "Row, Row, Row Your Boat"*)
Friendly words, friendly words,
Are so nice to say.
Friendly words, friendly words,
Make a friend today.

Skill Focus
Listening and Speaking
Phonological Awareness (Rhythm and Repetition)
Social and Emotional Awareness
Vocabulary

Theme Connection
Friends

Many Friends

AGE 4+

What to Do

- Ask the children to think of their friends. Ask, *How are your friends alike? How are they different?*
- Ask, *Who can be a friend? Can a girl and a boy be friends? Can you have more than one friend?*
- Emphasize that all kinds of people can be friends—brothers and sisters, cousins, people who speak different languages, people and their pets, and so on.
- Have the children stand in a circle and sing "Make New Friends."

    Make New Friends
    (*Tune: Traditional*)
    Make new friends,
    But keep the old.
    One is silver,
    The other is gold.

    A circle is round,
    It has no end.
    That's how long,
    I will be your friend.

    You have one hand,
    I have the other.
    Put them together, (*Children hold hands.*)
    We have each other.

- When you sing the third verse, have the children hold hands with the child on each side of them.

Vocabulary

alike   friend
boy   girl
circle   gold
different   silver

Materials

none needed

Click on the
Between the Lions website!
pbskids.org/lions/gryphonhouse

Stories:
- Owen and Mzee
- Yo! Yes?

Cleo and Theo's Book Suggestions

Bein' with You This Way
by W. Nikola-Lisa
A group of children playing together in the park celebrate their differences. [adapted for a *Between the Lions* episode]

Friends at School
by Rochelle Bunnett
Photographs and text tell the story of a diverse group of children, some with disabilities, who are friends at school.

How to Lose All Your Friends
by Nancy Carlson
This book tells what to do to make sure that you don't have any friends. In the process, children learn positive behaviors that help them make and get along with friends.

A Kid's Best Friend
by Maya Ajmera and Alex Fisher
Photographs show children around the world with their dogs.

Lissy's Friends by Grace Lin
Lissy is lonely on her first day of school, so she makes a bird from origami paper to keep her company. Soon she has a group of folded animal friends. When they blow away, a new friend comes to the rescue.

■ Talk with the children about what the song means. Emphasize that it's great to make new friends, but that doesn't mean that we give up our old friends.

Extension Idea

Teach the children "Friends at School," another song about friends.

Friends at School
(*Tune: "Frère Jacques"*)
I'm a good friend.
I'm a good friend.
So are you.
So are you.
We can play together.
We can learn together.
Friends at school.
Friends at school.

Skill Focus
Listening and Speaking
Vocabulary

Theme Connection
Helping

Everyone Needs Help

What to Do

- Engage the children in a discussion about helping others. Talk about what it means to help someone. Ask, *Has anyone ever asked you for help? Were you able to help? What did you do to help?*
- Read the book *The Lion and the Mouse*. Ask, *Why did the lion say a mouse couldn't help a lion?* Emphasize that everyone needs help sometimes—even grownups.
- Tell the children about a time when someone helped you. Then ask, *Have you ever helped a big person—a grownup or an older brother or sister? What did you do?*
- Talk about the importance of teamwork. *When we work together, we are a team. Teamwork helps us do a better job and makes the work go faster.* Ask, *What do we do together as a team that would be much harder for just one of us to do?*

Cleo and Theo's Book Suggestions

Fables from Aesop adapted and illustrated by Tom Lynch
"The Lion and the Mouse" is included in this collection of Aesop's fables.

Grandma Lena's Big Ol' Turnip by Denia Lewis Hester
This retelling of **The Gigantic Turnip** is about teamwork, sharing, and cooking in an extended African American family.

The Lion and the Mouse by Carol Jones
In this adaptation, an adventurous mouse leaves his home on a ship and saves the king of the jungle.

Vocabulary

ask	harder
brother	help
enormous	huge
everyone	older
faster	sister
giant	team
gigantic	teamwork
grownup	together

Material

The Lion and the Mouse by Bernadette Watts

Click on the *Between the Lions* website!
pbskids.org/lions/gryphonhouse

Story: The Lion and the Mouse

Making Music

Skill Focus
Listening and Speaking
Listening to Music
Vocabulary

Theme Connections
Music
Sounds

Vocabulary

bass	oboe
bassoon	sing
cello	tambourine
clarinet	triangle
drums	trombone
French horn	tuba
harmonica	viola
musical	violin
instruments	xylophone

Materials

classroom musical instruments, such as a xylophone, triangle, drums, and so on
pictures of traditional musical instruments, such as a violin, cello, tuba, clarinet, and so on, if possible

Click on the *Between the Lions* website!
pbskids.org/lions/gryphonhouse

Story: Violet's Music
Poem: Tuning Up
Game: Dub Cubs

What to Do

◻ Engage the children in a discussion about music and the songs that they like. Talk about what you and the children like about the music.

◻ Ask, *How do we make music?* Emphasize that we make music in many ways. Say, *We make music with our voices when we sing.* Have the children place their hands on their throats and feel the vibrations as you sing together: *La, la, la, la.*

◻ Tell the children that we also make music by playing musical instruments.

◻ Talk about the traditional musical instruments.

◻ Say, *There are many different kinds of musical instruments. Each has its own sound.* Pretend to play the drum and ask, *What musical instrument am I playing?*

◻ Have the class join you in pretending to play drums. Say, *A drum is a musical instrument you play by beating it with your hands or with sticks.*

◻ Ask a child to point out a drum.

◻ Encourage children to talk about other musical instruments they know, and then use the instrument to accompany a song that they know such as "Row, Row, Row Your Boat," "Twinkle, Twinkle, Little Star" or "The Wheels on the Bus."

Cleo and Theo's Book Suggestions

Ah, Music! by Aliki
   A beginner's guide to composers, instruments, artists, and performers, this book includes facts about music history and genres.

Violet's Music by Angela Johnson
   Violet plays music every chance she gets, and she's always looking for other kids who think and dream music all day long. [featured on a *Between the Lions* episode]

Skill Focus
Listening and Speaking
Vocabulary

Theme Connection
Music

Our Own Band!

Preparation
◼ Label a few containers with the children's names. These will be drums.
◼ Gather an assortment of other instruments, one per child (maracas, rubber-band guitars, cardboard-tube horns, and so on).
◼ Label each instrument with a child's name.

What to Do
◼ Talk with the children about what a band does. A *band* is a group that makes music together. The people who play music in the band are called *musicians*.
◼ Tell the children that Lionel and Leona have a band. Ask, *Would you like our class to have our own band? What musical instruments could we play in our band?*
◼ Review what each instrument is called. Then display the name tag on each instrument so each child can claim one.
◼ Help the children sort themselves into groups—children with the same instruments should sit together.
◼ Encourage the children to explore the sounds that the instruments can make, and then ask the children to play their instruments as you sing a familiar song ("Twinkle, Twinkle, Little Star," "Old MacDonald," "The Wheels on the Bus," or any other song that the children know and enjoy).

Cleo and Theo's Book Suggestions
Charlie Parker Played Be Bop by Chris Raschka
Shoes, birds, lollipops, and letters dance across the pages to the beat of Charlie Parker's saxophone music. [featured on a *Between the Lions* episode]

Music Is by Lloyd Moss and Philippe Petit-Roulet
A rhyming tribute to the many ways people enjoy music.

Vocabulary
band   music
instruments   musicians

Materials
assorted classroom instruments, such as maracas, rubber-band guitars, cardboard-tube horns, and so on
containers
labels
markers

Click on the *Between the Lions* website!
pbskids.org/lions/gryphonhouse

Story: What Instrument Does Alvin Play?
Poem: Tuning Up
Video Clip: Fred: Musical Instruments
Game: Dub Cubs

Neighborhood Places

Vocabulary

errand	person
family	place
Laundromat	post office
live	school
nearby	shopping
neighbor	task
neighborhood	trip
next door	

Materials

chart paper
markers

What to Do

- Engage the children in a discussion about their neighborhoods. Say, *A neighborhood is the place where you live. A neighbor is a person who lives next door or near you.*
- Talk about places in the children's neighborhoods and/or in the neighborhood around your school. Ask, *Which places in your neighborhood do you like to go to with your family? What do you do there?*
- Write the children's responses on chart paper. Label it *Neighborhood Places.*

Extension Idea

Talk about errands. Explain that an *errand* is a short trip to do a task, like going to a Laundromat, a post office, or shopping. Ask, *Have you ever gone shopping with your mom or dad? How did you get there? What did you do? Do you like going on errands with your family?*

Skill Focus
Listening and Speaking
Vocabulary

Theme Connection
My Neighborhood

Going to the Library

AGE 3+

What to Do

- Tell the children that one of your favorite places to visit is your neighborhood library: *I love going to the library because there are so many great books there for me to read!*
- Ask the children, *Have you ever been to a library? What did you see at the library? What did you do? What did you like best about it?*
- Explain that the lion family— parents Theo and Cleo with their cubs, Lionel and Leona—live in a library.

- Talk about different kinds of libraries that the children may be familiar with: the Library Center in your classroom, the *Between the Lions* library, and the public library.
- Continue to talk with individual children throughout the day about their experiences with libraries and books.

Extension Idea

Suggest that the children dictate a story about an experience they had at a library.

Vocabulary

books	love
family	neighborhood
favorite	place
library	visit
lion	

Materials

none needed

Click on the *Between the Lions* website!
pbskids.org/lions/gryphonhouse

Song: Library A to Z

All Kinds of Books

Vocabulary

books	kind
different	library
DVDs	magazines
family	neighborhood
favorite	newspapers
fiction	nonfiction
find	variety
how-to	

Materials

none needed

Preparation

☐ Bring in samples of different books and other materials from a library.

What to Do

☐ Remind the children about what libraries are and how they are part of a neighborhood.

☐ Tell the children that you are going to talk about all the different kinds of books and other things that can be found at a library.

☐ Ask, *What kinds of books can you find at a library?* Display a variety of books, including nonfiction books and how-to books. Say, *A library has all kinds of books: storybooks, books about real things such as rockets and frogs, books that tell you how to build things, and books that help you learn how to cook. A library also has magazines, newspapers, books on tape, and DVDs.*

☐ Show the children the samples of materials from your library that you brought to class.

Extension Idea

Use chart paper and markers to create a list of the children's favorite books and then, over a period ot time, read the books on the list.

Click on the *Between the Lions* website! pbskids.org/lions/gryphonhouse

Song: Read a Book Today!

Theme Connection
My Neighborhood

Reasons to Read

**AGE
4+**

What to Do

- Talk with the children about all the different kinds of books they can find at the library. Have them name some.
- Ask, *What reasons do we have to read?* Explain that reasons are why we do something. Tell the children that one reason we read stories is because they are fun and enjoyable. Another reason we read is to find information about things we are curious about, such as airplanes or frogs.
- Ask, *How does reading help you?*
- Encourage the children to think and talk about different reasons to read.
- Continue to talk with the individual children throughout the day about the different ways reading helps us in our lives.

Extension Idea

Write the children's responses on a Reasons to Read chart. Read the completed chart together. Save the chart to add to throughout the year as the children discover new reasons to read.

Vocabulary

borrow	read
find	reasons
information	response
librarian	return
library card	why

Materials

none needed

Click on the
*Between the
Lions* website!
pbskids.org/lions/gryphonhouse

Song: Got a Good Reason to Read

Sleep

Skill Focus
Health Awareness
Listening and Speaking
Vocabulary

Theme Connection
Nighttime

Vocabulary

bedtime story   nightlight
blanket   nighttime
lullaby   sleep
night   stuffed animal

Materials

blankets
favorite stuffed animal or object

What to Do

☐ Invite the children to gather in a circle with blankets and a favorite stuffed animal or object.

☐ Dim the lights to create a nighttime mood.

☐ Invite the children to talk about their nighttime routines.

☐ Ask, *What do you do before you go to sleep at night?* Talk about things that help the children fall asleep (bedtime story, special stuffed animal, hug, lullaby, nightlight, and so on).

☐ Emphasize that everyone needs to sleep. *When we sleep, our bodies and minds grow strong. After a good night's sleep, our bodies and minds are ready to play and to learn.*

Cleo and Theo's Book Suggestions

Goodnight Moon by Margaret Wise Brown and Clement Hurd
    In this classic bedtime story, a young rabbit says goodnight to each of the objects in his room.

Grandfather Twilight by Barbara Helen Berger
    Grandfather Twilight goes for a walk through the woods as the day draws to a close.

Here Comes the Night by Anne Rockwell
    In this soothing story, a mother and son go through their nighttime ritual.

Sleepy Bears by Mem Fox and Kerry Argent
    Six cubs refuse to settle down until their mother recites a unique rhyming tale that soothes each one.

Click on the *Between the Lions* website!
pbskids.org/lions/gryphonhouse

Story: Tabby Cat at Night

Skill Focus
Concepts of Print
Listening and Speaking
Using Senses
Vocabulary

Theme Connections
Nighttime
Sounds

Night Sounds

What to Do

- ▣ Talk with the children about nighttime. You might say, *Nighttime is a quiet time. It's a time to rest and to sleep. But if we listen carefully we can hear noises, or sounds.*
- ▣ Ask the children to close their eyes and imagine that it is night and they are in their beds ready to go to sleep.
- ▣ Ask, *What sounds do you hear before you go to sleep at night?*
- ▣ List the children's responses on chart paper under the heading *Night Sounds.*
- ▣ Ask, *Do you sometimes feel afraid when you hear a sound at night and you don't know what it is?*
- ▣ Assure the children that when we know what makes the sound it helps us feel less afraid.
- ▣ On the same day or another day, talk to the children about bedtime. You might say, *I like bedtime when I put my son to sleep. We cuddle and I sing him a song that my mother used to sing to me when I was little. Then I read a story. By then he's tired and falls asleep.*
- ▣ Ask, *Do you like to listen to a story at bedtime? What do you do at bedtime to help you fall asleep?*

Cleo and Theo's Book Suggestions

All the Pretty Little Horses by Linda Saport
   Beautiful pastel illustrations highlight this classic lullaby.

Bedtime for Little Bears! by David Bedford and Caroline Pedler
   When a polar bear cub refuses to go to sleep, his mother takes
   him for a walk so he can see how other animals prepare for bed.

Sleep, Black Bear, Sleep
   by Jane Yolen, Heidi Y. Stemple, and Brooke Dyer
   Rhyming text tells how a variety of animals settle down for their
   winter naps.

Vocabulary

afraid	quiet
bedtime	rest
listen	sleep
nighttime	sounds
noises	story

Materials

chart paper
markers

Click on the
*Between the
Lions* website!
pbskids.org/lions/gryphonhouse

Story: Night in the Country

Four Seasons Fun

Skill Focus
Listening and Speaking
Understanding the Natural
World
Vocabulary

Theme Connection
Seasons

Vocabulary

asleep	hibernation
autumn	seasons
awake	snow
bear	spring
clothes	summer
fall	wear
hibernate	winter

Materials

Seasons wall display (see Setting Up the Room, page 19)

Click on the *Between the Lions* website!
pbskids.org/lions/gryphonhouse

Story: Winter Is the Warmest Season

Poems:
- Big Snow
- Four Seasons
- Little Seeds

Video Clips:
- Cliff Hanger and the Giant Snail
- Joy Learno: snowman
- Summer is fun in Alaska!

What to Do

- Show the children the Seasons wall display.
- Explain that there are four different **seasons** in the year: winter, spring, summer, and fall, or autumn. Help the children begin to understand that the seasons are different in different climates: winter is warmer in Florida and California than it is in New York, for example.
- Point to the pictures of a season and discuss what takes place in that season.
- Talk about all four seasons, or spread out the discussion over a series of days.

Winter Fun

- Look at the pictures on the Seasons wall display.
- Say, *Winter is the coldest season.* If children have not experienced snow, explain that in some places it gets so cold in the winter that rain turns to snows. *Snow is small white pieces of ice that fall to the ground. Snow can be very beautiful. It can also be very fluffy. Children like to play in the snow. They make snowballs and snowmen and slide down hills covered in snow.*
- Talk about the winter pictures on the Seasons wall display.
- Ask, *What are some things you like to do in the winter? What clothes do you wear in the winter?*

Spring Fun

- Look at the pictures on the Seasons wall display. Remind the children that there are four seasons: winter, spring, summer, and fall.
- Say, *Bears sleep or hibernate all winter long. They wake up when it is warm again.*
- Ask, *Which season is it when they wake up? Yes, it's spring.*

- Talk about the spring pictures on the Seasons wall display.
- Emphasize that it rains a lot in some places in spring. Plants and flowers grow in spring.
- Ask, *What are some things you like to do in the spring? What clothes do you wear in the spring?*

Summer Fun

- Look at the pictures on the Seasons wall display. Remind the children that there are four seasons: winter, spring, summer, and fall.
- Ask, *In which season do plants and flowers start to grow? Yes, spring!* Then ask, *What is the hottest season of the year? Summer is the hottest season of the year. It comes after spring.*
- Talk about the summer pictures on the Seasons wall display.
- Ask, *What are some things you like to do in the summer? What clothes do you wear in the summer?*

Fall Fun

- Look at the pictures on the Seasons wall display. Remind the children that there are four seasons: winter, spring, summer, and fall.
- Ask, *What is the hottest season?* Say, *Yes, summer is the hottest season. After summer, the days grow cooler. In some places, the leaves change color and fall off the trees. The season that comes after summer is called fall, or autumn.*
- Talk about the fall pictures on the Seasons wall display.
- Ask, *What are some things you like to do in the fall? What clothes do you wear in the fall?* Then ask, *What season comes after fall? Winter! After fall, it's winter again—then spring, then summer, then fall.*

Cleo and Theo's Book Suggestions

Animals in Winter
by Henrietta Bancroft and Helen K. Davie
Simple, factual text and illustrations show what animals do in the winter.

Come On, Rain!
by Karen Hesse and Jon J. Muth
In the middle of the summer heat, a girl gathers her friends to wait for the long-awaited rain.

Hurray for Spring!
by Patricia Hubbell
A boy celebrates spring's arrival by doing a variety of activities.

Thirteen Moons on Turtle's Back: A Native American Year of Moons by Joseph Bruchac and Jonathan London
Native American poems celebrate the passing of a year.

Winter Is the Warmest Season by Lauren Stringer
For the boy in this story, hot chocolate, fuzzy boots, and hissing radiators make winter the warmest season. [featured on a *Between the Lions* episode]

Listening Game

Skill Focus
Phonological Awareness
(Environmental Sounds)

Theme Connections
Sounds
My Neighborhood

Vocabulary

ears	recognize
environment	sound
hear	tell me
listen	

Materials

none needed

What to Do

- Play a game to help the children listen to and recognize sounds in their environment.
- Ask the children to close their eyes.
- Recite:

> Listen, listen with your ears.
> Tell me, tell me what you hear!

- Make a sound (clap your hands, tap your feet, ring a bell, close a door, and so on).
- Ask the children to guess what the sound is.

Note: You can also play this game with tape-recorded sounds.

Cleo and Theo's Book Suggestions

City Lullaby by Marilyn Singer and Carll Cneut
Lively poems transform the sounds of the city into a lullaby for a sleepy baby.

The Listening Walk by Paul Showers and Aliki
A girl and her father take a special walk and listen to the sounds around them.

Night in the Country by Cynthia Rylant
Lyrical text and rich, color-pencil drawings shine a light on the activities and sounds that happen in the dark. [featured on a *Between the Lions* episode]

Sounds All Around by Wendy Pfeffer and Holly Keller
This nonfiction book in the Let's-Read-and-Find-Out Science series offers a simple explanation of sounds and hearing, including how animals hear.

Sounds of the Wild: Nighttime by Maurice Pledger
This nonfiction book describes sounds made by night animals in different parts of the world.

Skill Focus
Listening and Speaking
(Expressing Opinions)
Vocabulary

Theme Connections
Sounds
My Neighborhood

Loud Noises

What to Do

- Discuss how the children feel about loud noises.
- Ask, *What are some loud noises that we hear?* You may want to give some prompts: *Imagine you are on a street with lots of cars. What loud noises might you hear? Think of things in your home that are loud. Think of animals that are loud.*
- Record the children's responses on chart paper.
- Tell the children that sometimes loud sounds can be happy and exciting. At other times, loud sounds can be scary, upsetting, or unpleasant.
- Read the list of sounds on the chart and ask the children to think about which sounds they like and which ones they do not. You may want to draw a happy face next to sounds that the children like and a sad face next to sounds they do not.

Extension Idea

Engage the children in a discussion about the the loud noises they like and don't like that are recorded on the Loud Noises chart. Or create a class chart of the children's favorite sounds.

Vocabulary

audience	stomp
exciting	unpleasant
happy	upsetting
scary	vibrate
stage voice	

Materials

chart paper
markers

Click on the
*Between the
Lions* website!
pbskids.org/lions/gryphonhouse

Song: Very Loud, Very Big,
Very Metal

Video Clips:
- Opposite Bunny: loud/quiet
- The Amazing Trampolini Brothers: noisy, noisier, noisiest

Loud Times, Quiet Times

Skill Focus
Listening and Speaking
Vocabulary

Theme Connections
Sounds
Opposites

Vocabulary

big	quiet
gentle	quieter
loud	rehearsals
louder	soft
magnificent	storm
play	strong

Materials

none needed

What to Do

▣ Help the children explore the concepts of *loud* and *quiet*. Say, *When we are* loud, *we speak in big, strong voices. When we are* quiet, *we speak in soft, gentle voices.*

▣ Invite the children to say "Hooray!" first in a very loud voice and then in a very quiet voice.

▣ Ask, *When is it okay to be loud?* Encourage a wide variety of responses: at the playground or park, on stage during a show, cheering during a game.

▣ Ask, *When is it good to be quiet?* (in their home, when people are sleeping, at a library, in a restaurant) Observe that loud voices are often used outdoors and soft voices are often used indoors.

Cleo and Theo's Book Suggestions

The Listening Walk by Paul Showers and Aliki
A girl and her father take a special walk and listen to the sounds around them.

Ruby Sings the Blues by Niki Daly
Ruby's voice is SO loud, it's driving everyone crazy, until her jazz-playing neighbors come up with a plan and Ruby learns to sing without everyone needing earplugs. [featured on a *Between the Lions* episode]

Sounds All Around by Wendy Pfeffer and Holly Keller
This book in the Let's-Read-and-Find-Out Science series offers a simple explanation of sounds and hearing, including how animals hear.

Click on the *Between the Lions* website!
pbskids.org/lions/gryphonhouse

Story: Ruby Sings the Blues
Video Clips:

▣ Opposite Bunny: loud/quiet

▣ The Amazing Trampolini Brothers: noisy, noisier, noisiest

Skill Focus

Following Directions

Listening to Musical Instruments

Vocabulary

Theme Connections

Sounds

Weather

Drum Up a Storm

What to Do

■ Talk with the children about storms and the noises they hear in storms. Say, *When a storm is close, the wind and rain and thunder are very loud.* (Demonstrate by beating your drum loudly.) *When the storm moves away, it gets quieter and quieter until you can hardly hear it at all.* (Demonstrate by beating your drum more and more softly, until you can hardly hear the sound.)

■ Invite the children to drum up their storms. Distribute pots, containers, boxes, and pails to the children to use as drums. Say, *First the storm is far away. You can just barely hear it in the distance.* Drum very, very quietly. Say, *Now the storm is coming closer. It's getting louder.* Drum a little louder. Say, *Now the storm is right on top of us. It's very loud.* Drum as loud as you can. Say, *That is quite a storm! Now it's quieting down and moving away. Let's drum a little more quietly, and even more quietly, and now as quietly as you can. Now stop.*

Cleo and Theo's Book Suggestion

Walter Was Worried by Laura Vaccaro Seeger

This alphabet book explores children's emotional reactions to a storm.

Vocabulary

away	quiet
drum	quieter
hear	rain
loud	softly
louder	storms
noises	thunder

Materials

pots, containers, boxes, and pails to use as drums

Chapter 3

Learning to Appreciate and Love Books

This chapter of *Wild About Literacy* focuses on ways to help children learn to appreciate and love books. Reading to small groups of children or individual children is a great way to help them develop an appreciation for books and discover the joys of reading (see The Literacy Scope and Sequence on pages 14–15). Children enjoy many different kinds of books, including favorite folktales, rhyming books, alphabet books, and concept books. Children develop an appreciation for books and learn what books have to offer when you read to them with joy and enthusiasm.

The activities in this chapter are grouped alphabetically by topic and then by age (3+ or 4+) within each topic or theme. The activities have the following components:

Skill Focus	**Materials**
Theme Connection(s)	**Preparation (if necessary)**
Vocabulary	**What to Do**

Skill Focus—lists the literacy skills that the activity addresses and other skills that young children need to learn, such as fine motor skills or emotional awareness.

Theme Connections—lists one or two familiar early childhood themes that the activity covers. If more than one theme is listed, the first is the one with the strongest connection.

Vocabulary—lists words that are part of the activity. Use these when you are engaging children in the activity, defining their meaning if necessary. Repeat these words throughout the day so children hear the words used in context and can begin to understand how each word is used.

Materials—lists, in alphabetical order, the materials you will need to do the activity. Be sure you have the materials you need before you begin the activity.

A Note About Repetition: You will find the same songs, poems, and books used in multiple activities in *Wild About Literacy*. Children benefit and learn from repetition. When children hear a familiar song or poem, they may learn something new or solidify what they already know. Using a familiar song or story to teach a new skill is a technique used by many teachers, which is why you will find repetition in this book.

Preparation—If the activity needs any preparation, such as writing a song or poem on chart paper or preparing a chart, what you need to do is described in this section.

What to Do—Step by step, this section outlines how to engage children in the activity.

In addition, many activities include ideas that build on the main activity, extend it to another curriculum area, or suggest books that relate to the activity.

The following children's books are used in one or more activities in this chapter:

David's Drawings by Cathryn Falwell (see page 69)

How Many Stars in the Sky? by Lenny Hort (see page 72)

Joseph Had a Little Overcoat by Simms Tabach (see page 68)
    [featured on a *Between the Lions* episode]

My Crayons Talk by G. Brian Karas (see page 69)

The Seals on the Bus
    by G. Brian Karas (see page 69)

In addition, the following children's books are suggested as a way to extend an activity:

City Lullaby by Marilyn Singer and Carll Cneut

The Night Worker by Kate Banks and Georg Hallensleben

Click on the
Between the Lions website!
pbskids.org/lions/gryphonhouse

Books About Reading
Books Featured on *Between the Lions*
Recommended Books

"Read, Read, Read a Book"

AGE 4+

What to Do

⊡ Sing "Read, Read, Read a Book."

Read, Read, Read a Book
(*Tune: "Row, Row, Row Your Boat"*)
Read, read, read a book
Every single day.
Merrily, merrily, merrily, merrily
Every single day.

⊡ Add motion to the song by opening your hands and pretending to hold and read a book.
⊡ Invite the children to sing along with you.

Extension Idea

Teach the children "This Is the Way We Hold Our Books."

This Is the Way We Hold Our Books
(*Tune: "Lazy Mary"*)
This is the way we hold our books,
Hold our books, hold our books.
This is the way we hold our books
When we are busy reading.

This is the way we open our books,
Open our books, open our books.
This is the way we open our books
When we are busy reading.

This is the way we turn a page,
Turn a page, turn a page.
This is the way we turn a page
When we are busy reading.

Vocabulary

book	merrily
day	open
every	read
hold	

Materials

none needed

Click on the
Between the Lions website!
pbskids.org/lions/gryphonhouse

Song: Read a Book Today!

Joseph Had a Little Overcoat

Skill Focus
Book Appreciation (Illustrations)
Concepts of Print
Environmental Print
Interpreting Illustrations
Vocabulary

Theme Connection
Clothing

Vocabulary

chorus	scarf
cutout	sewing
details	sewing
handkerchief	machine
illustrations	spool of
letters	thread
necktie	vest
needle	worn
overcoat	Yiddish

Materials

Joseph Had a Little Overcoat by Simms Tabach

Click on the *Between the Lions* website!
pbskids.org/lions/gryphonhouse

Story: Joseph Had a Little Overcoat

What to Do

- Read aloud *Joseph Had a Little Overcoat* to individuals or small groups.
- Invite the children to chime in on the repeating phrases in the book.
- Point to the illustrations to help clarify the meaning of unfamiliar words, such as *overcoat, worn, vest, scarf, chorus, necktie,* and *handkerchief.*
- Look at the cutouts in the book together and let the children feel them. Show how a shape reveals what Joseph will make next. Discuss how the cutout blends in with the illustration and can be hard to see until you lift a page. Talk about what you see through the cutout on the right and left side of a page.
- Linger over each page to allow the children time to explore the fun details in the art. For example, ask the children to find and name the animals, vegetables, sewing, and art tools. Have them describe the marvelous hats!
- Point out and read some of the environmental print in the artwork, such as letters, postcards, photographs, newspapers, food labels, books, and sheet music. Explain that some of the written words are Yiddish, a language spoken by Jewish people. The letters in the Yiddish language look very different from letters in English.

Extension Idea

Suggest that the children look at the illustrations with a magnifying glass. See if they can find Joseph's color chart on the final spread when he makes his book!

Skill Focus

Book Appreciation (Illustrator's Style)

Compare and Contrast

Making Connections (Between Books)

Theme Connection

Colors

Illustrators Have Style

What to Do

- Engage the children in a discussion about styles of art, pointing out that each artist has a different style.
- Tell the children that an artist's *style* is a special look that lets you recognize that person's artwork.
- Display a group of four to six books, including two or three illustrated by Cathryn Falwell (see page 213). Say, *Cathryn Falwell has her own style. Let's see if you can pick out some other books that she has illustrated.* Ask, *What do you notice about Cathryn Falwell's style that is the same in these books? What do you like about her illustrations?*
- On the same day, or on another day, display a variety of picture books illustrated by different artists, including books illustrated by G. Brian Karas (see page 213).
- Ask the children if they can pick out the books that G. Brian Karas has illustrated. Ask, *What do you notice about his style that is the same in these books? What do you like about his illustrations?*

Extension Idea

Ask the children to describe something that they like about the art of Cathryn Falwell or G. Brian Karas. Write their responses on chart paper.

Vocabulary

author   illustrator

illustrations   style

Materials

picture books with art by a variety of illustrators

two or three books illustrated by Cathryn Falwell such as *David's Drawings* (see page 213 for more suggestions)

two or three books illustrated by G. Brian Karas, such as *My Crayons Talk* and *The Seals on the Bus* (see page 213 for more suggestions)

Taking Care of Books

Skill Focus
Book Appreciation
Listening and Speaking
Vocabulary

Theme Connections
My Neighborhood

Vocabulary

borrow	open
conversation	over and over
favorite	read
find	reasons
hold	response
information	return
librarian	take care of
library card	turn a page
look at	why

Materials

none needed

What to Do

☑ Display the Reasons to Read chart (page 55) or create one.

☑ Begin or review conversations you have had with the children about all the reasons we have to read.

☑ Talk about or remind the children about how to take care of books. Ask:

  ☑ *How do we take care of books?*

  ☑ *How do you open a book?*

  ☑ *Who has a favorite book that they like to read over and over again?*

  ☑ *How would you feel if someone borrowed your favorite book and drew all over it?*

☑ Have the children show you how to hold a book, turn a page, and look at a book with a friend. Then ask, *Where do you place books when you have finished reading them? Show me.*

Extension Idea

Help the children develop a list of how to care for books. Ask, *What rules can we make about how to take care of the books in our library?* List the children's responses on a chart. Add your recommendations. Read the completed chart with the children. Add illustrations to help the children "read" the chart on their own. Display the chart in the Library Center.

Click on the
*Between the
Lions* website!
pbskids.org/lions/gryphonhouse

Song: Got a Good Reason
  to Read

Hunting for Books

AGE 4+

What to Do

- Before singing the song, remind the children that a library has many different kinds of books.
- Ask, *What are your favorite books?* Encourage a wide variety of responses by showing children different kinds of books from the classroom library.
- Tell the children that you are going to sing a song about going on a "book hunt." Teach the children a variation of "A-Hunting We Will Go."

> **A-Hunting We Will Go**
> (*Tune: Traditional*)
> A-hunting we will go,
> A-hunting we will go.
> We'll find ourselves a favorite book,
> And then to home we'll go.

- After singing it a few times, invite the children to change the words "favorite book" in the song to another kind of book—a fairy tale, lion book, storybook, and so on.
- Name some of the children's favorite books. Then have the children sing the song as they hunt for the books in the classroom library.

Extension Idea

Before the children arrive, hide familiar books in different parts of the classroom. Challenge the children to find the books that you have hidden. Say, *Look for the book about lions that we read yesterday.*

Vocabulary

books	find
classroom	hunt
different	hunting
favorite	library

Materials

books from the classroom library

Click on the *Between the Lions* website!
pbskids.org/lions/gryphonhouse

Song: Read a Book Today!

How Many Stars in the Sky?

Skill Focus
Book Appreciation
Concepts of Print
Story Comprehension
Vocabulary

Theme Connections
Nighttime
Stars

Vocabulary

Big Dipper	Milky Way
blinked	neon signs
bright	planet
city	searchlights
country	skyline
department store	skyscrapers
displays	stars
distance	street lamp
flashed	streetlights
gazing	treehouse
headlights	tunnel
Jupiter	underneath

Materials

How Many Stars in the Sky? by Lenny Hort

Click on the *Between the Lions* website!
pbskids.org/lions/gryphonhouse

Song: Shower of Stars

What to Do

- Read aloud *How Many Stars in the Sky?* to individuals or small groups.
- Use the illustrations in the book to help the children understand the meaning of words such as *tree house, streetlights, skyline, tunnel, department store, displays, street lamps, neon signs, headlights,* and *skyscrapers*.
- Point out the environmental print, such as the No Parking sign.
- Talk about how many different kinds of lights are shown in the book: streetlights, street lamps, searchlights, headlights, and neon signs.
- Talk about how we use lights at night to help us see.
- Before you read the last page, ask the children to predict which star the boy and his dad could see in the morning.
- After reading the book, ask the children why the boy and his dad couldn't see the stars very well in the city. Talk about where the children live. Do they live in a city, a town, or the country? Can they see the stars at night from their house?

Cleo and Theo's Book Suggestions

City Lullaby by Marilyn Singer and Carll Cneut
Lively poems transform the sounds of the city into a lullaby for a sleepy baby.

The Night Worker by Kate Banks and Georg Hallensleben
A boy goes to work with his father, a construction engineer who works at night.

Chapter 4

Learning to Understand Stories

The activities in this chapter of *Wild About Literacy* focus on building a strong foundation in story comprehension to help children become good readers. Use these activities to create opportunities for children to make connections between stories and their lives and to predict what will happen next in a story. Learning to understand the meaning of stories, to retell stories, and to compare and contrast stories are essential building block of literacy (see The Literacy Scope and Sequence on pages 14–15). Use the following activities to help children deepen their knowledge and comprehension of stories.

The activities in this chapter are grouped by topic and then by age (3+ or 4+) within each theme, and have the following components:

Skill Focus	Materials
Theme Connection(s)	Preparation (if necessary)
Vocabulary	What to Do

Skill Focus—lists the literacy skills that the activity addresses and other skills that young children need to learn, such as fine motor skills or emotional awareness.

Theme Connections—lists one or two familiar early childhood themes that the activity covers. If more than one theme is listed, the first is the one with the strongest connection.

Vocabulary—lists words that are part of the activity. Use these when you are engaging children in the activity, defining their meaning if necessary. Repeat these words throughout the day so children hear the words used in context and can begin to understand how each word is used.

Materials—lists, in alphabetical order, the materials you will need to do the activity. Be sure you have the materials you need before you begin the activity.

Preparation—If the activity needs any preparation, such as writing a song or poem on chart paper or preparing a chart, what you need to do is described in this section.

A Note About Repetition: You will find the same songs, poems, and books used in multiple activities in *Wild About Literacy*. Children benefit and learn from repetition. When children hear a familiar song or poem, they may learn something new or solidify what they already know. Using a familiar song or story to teach a new skill is a technique used by many teachers, which is why you will find repetition in this book.

What to Do—Step by step, this section outlines how to engage children in the activity.

In addition, many activities include ideas that build on the main activity, extend it to another curriculum area, or suggest books that relate to the activity.

The following children's books are used in one or more activities in this chapter:

A Letter to Amy by Ezra Jack Keats (see page 82)

Bunny Cakes by Rosemary Wells (see page 80)

The Enormous Potato
   by Aubrey Davis and Dusan Petricic (see pages 84 and 89)

Good Night, Gorilla by Peggy Rathmann (see page 86)

Hush! A Thai Lullaby by Minfong Ho and Holly Meade (see page 76)

I Miss You, Stinky Face by Lisa McCourt and Cyd Moore
   (see page 76) [featured on a *Between the Lions* episode]

Jonathan and His Mommy by Irene Smalls (see page 78)

Knuffle Bunny by Mo Willems (see page 78)
   [featured on a *Between the Lions* episode]

The Lion and the Mouse by Bernadette Watts (see page 84)

My Friends by Taro Gomi (see page 82)

Night in the Country by Cynthia Rylant and mary Szilagyi (see page
   77) [featured on a *Between the Lions* episode]

Owl Babies by Martin Waddell and Patrick Benson (see page 79)

Too Many Tamales by Gary Soto (see page 81)

Yo! Yes? by Chris Raschka (see page 82) [featured on a *Between the
   Lions* episode]

In addition, many children's books are suggested as a way to extend an
   activity. Some of the book suggestions in this chapter include:

Arrorró, Mi Niño: Latino Lullabies and Gentle Games
   by Lulu Delacre

Buzz by Janet S. Wong and Margaret Chodos-Irvine

Cucumber Soup by Vickie Leigh Krudwig and Craig McFarland Brown

Grandma Lena's Big Ol' Turnip
   by Denia Lewis Hester and Jackie Urbanovic

The Happy Hocky Family by Lane Smith

How Chipmunk Got His Stripes
   by Joseph and James Bruchac, Jose Aruego, and Ariane Dewey

I Love You Because You're You by Liz Baker

Kevin and His Dad by Irene Smalls

Mama, Do You Love Me? by Barbara Joosse and Barbara Lavallee

The Very Best Daddy of All by Marion Dane Bauer and Leslie Wu

We Are Best Friends by Aliki

Click on the
*Between the
Lions* website!
pbskids.org/lions/gryphonhouse

Books About Reading
Books Featured on *Between
   the Lions*
Recommended Books
Stories: Animated videos of
stories featured on *Between
the Lions*

Telling Stories

Skill Focus
Imaginative Play
Storytelling
Vocabulary

Theme Connections
Animals
Storytelling

What to Do

- Divide the class or small groups into buddies (see page 17).
- Encourage the buddies to use puppets or play people and animals to tell each other stories.
- Ask the children to retell stories (for example, "The Lion and the Mouse" or "the Three Little Pigs") or books (for example, *We Are Best Friends* by Aliki or *Yo! Yes?* by Christopher Raschka) that are familiar to them, or they can mix up animal figures from different stories to make up friendship tales.
- Ask questions to help the children tell their stories: *What are your animal friends' names? What are they doing? What are they saying? Where are they going? Are they new friends or old friends?*

Cleo and Theo's Book Suggestions

A Kid's Best Friend by Maya Ajmera and Alex Fisher
Photographs show children around the world with their dogs.

Knuffle Bunny Too: A Case of Mistaken Identity
by Mo Willems
Trixie is excited to bring Knuffle Bunny to her first day at preschool, until she sees Sonja with a Knuffle Bunny of her own. After a bunny mix-up, the girls become friends.

Little Blue and Little Yellow
by Leo Lionni
A blue dot and a yellow dot are best friends. One day when they hug, they become a green dot.

We Are Best Friends
by Aliki
When a boy's best friend moves away, he learns that he can make new friends and still be loyal to his best one.

Vocabulary

animals	old
buddies	story
friends	tale
new	

Materials

puppets, play people and animals (pigs, wolves, owls, mice, lions, hens, cats, dogs, ducks, gorillas, and so on)
writing materials

Click on the *Between the Lions* website!
pbskids.org/lions/gryphonhouse

Story: Oh, Yes, It Can!

Hush! A Thai Lullaby

Skill Focus
Environmental Sounds
Interpreting Illustrations
Vocabulary

Theme Connections
Animals
Nighttime

Vocabulary

beeping	rice
breeze	shrieking
ceiling	sniffling
creeping	squeaking
dozes	sty
forest	sweeping
hay	swinging
hush	Thailand
leaping	water buffalo
lizard	weeping
lullaby	well
mosquito	wide awake
nearby	windowsill
peeping	

Material

Hush! A Thai Lullaby by Minfong
  Ho and Holly Meade

What to Do

☒ Read aloud *Hush! A Thai Lullaby* to individuals or small groups. Make the reading interactive:

☒ Pause to encourage the children to join the refrains in the book.

☒ Together, make the noises of the different animals.

☒ The baby appears on almost every spread. (Sometimes you can only see his feet.) Ask the children to look for and point to the baby and say whether he is asleep or awake.

☒ Use the illustrations to help the children understand the meaning of words such as *mosquito, lizard, hay, water buffalo,* and *windowsill.*

☒ Use motions and your voice to demonstrate the meaning of action and sound words such as *peeping, weeping, creeping, squeaking, leaping, sniffling, beeping, swinging, sweeping, shrieking,* and *dozes.*

Cleo and Theo's Book Suggestions

All the Pretty Little Horses by Linda Saport
  Beautiful pastel illustrations highlight this classic lullaby.

Arrorró, Mi Niño: Latino Lullabies and Gentle Games
  by Lulu Delacre
  A collection of lullabies and fingerplays from various Latin American countries.

Hush, Little Baby by Brian Pinkney
  In this version of the classic lullaby, Dad does what he can to soothe his young daughter while Mama does errands.

Twinkle, Twinkle, Little Star by Jane Taylor and Sylvia Long
  Watercolor pictures of young animals gazing at the stars and returning home to their parents illustrate the verses of the traditional lullaby.

Skill Focus

Active Listening
Making Connections
Story Comprehension
Vocabulary

Theme Connections

Animals
Nighttime

Night in the Country

What to Do

◻ Read aloud *Night in the Country* to individuals or small groups.

◻ Point out the setting sun on the cover and the title page.

◻ Have the children name the animals on each page.

◻ Use the illustrations, gestures, and sound effects to help the children understand the meaning of unfamiliar words such as *fields, swoop, clinks, creaking, patter, groan, thump, squeaks,* and *nuzzles.*

◻ After reading the book, invite the children to make some of the night noises (*reek, reek, groan, thump,* and *squeak*).

Extension Idea

Encourage the children to make connections between the story and their lives. Ask, *What do you hear when you go to sleep at night?*

Vocabulary

asleep	nuzzles
calf	owls
clinks	patter
creaking	rabbits
fields	raccoon
frogs	squeaks
groan	sunrise
late	sunset
licks	swoop
morning	thump
night	tractor

Material

Night in the Country by Cynthia Rylant and Mary Szilagyi

Click on the *Between the Lions* website!
pbskids.org/lions/gryphonhouse

Story: Night in the Country

Two Books About Families

Skill Focus
Making Connections
Story Comprehension

Theme Connections
Families
Helping

Vocabulary

books	feel
connect	feelings
connections	fun
dad	lost
family	mommy
favorite	read

Materials

Jonathan and His Mommy by Irene Smalls

Knuffle Bunny by Mo Willems

Click on the *Between the Lions* website!
pbskids.org/lions/gryphonhouse

Stories:

- ☑ Just What Mama Needs
- ☑ My Dog Is As Smelly As Dirty Socks

What to Do

☑ Display *Knuffle Bunny* and *Jonathan and His Mommy*.

☑ Ask questions such as the ones following to help the children make connections between themselves and the books they have read:

- ☑ *Trixie helps her dad wash the laundry. What do you help your family do?*
- ☑ *What does Jonathan like to do with his mommy? What are some fun things you like to do with your family?*
- ☑ *Trixie has a favorite stuffed animal. How does she feel when she loses it? Do you have a favorite stuffed animal? Have you ever lost it?*

Cleo and Theo's Book Suggestions

Buzz by Janet S. Wong and Margaret Chodos-Irvine
An Asian American child watches as his mommy and daddy get ready for work.

Count the Ways, Little Brown Bear
by Jonathan London and Masrgie Moore
Mama Brown Bear assures her cub how much she loves him in this bedtime counting book.

Grandfather and I by Helen Buckley and Jan Ormerod
A child tenderly relates how Grandfather is the perfect person to spend time with because he is never in a hurry. Also by the same author: ***Grandmother and I.***

Just What Mama Needs by Sharlee Mullins Glenn and Amiko Hirao
Abby loves dressing up in different costumes, and her mom enjoys finding ways a pirate, a detective, and a genie can help with chores around the house each day of the week. [featured on a *Between the Lions* episode]

Mama, Do You Love Me? by Barbara Joosse and Barbara Lavallee
A child living in the Artic learns that a mother's love is unconditional.

Skill Focus
Compare and Contrast
Listening and Speaking
Story Comprehension
Vocabulary

Theme Connections
Feelings
Families

Two Books About Feelings

What to Do

- Read *I Miss You, Stinky Face* and *Owl Babies* to the children.
- Ask questions such as the ones following to help the children make connections between the books they have read and themselves:
  - *When the owl mommy is away, how do her babies feel? Do they feel scared or safe?*
  - *How do the owl babies feel when their mommy comes home? How do you feel when you see your mommy after school?*
  - *When Stinky Face's mommy is away on her trip, how does he feel? Does he feel lonely or happy? How does he feel when she comes home?*

Cleo and Theo's Book Suggestions

Count the Ways, Little Brown Bear by Jonathan London
Mama Brown Bear assures her cub how much she loves him in this bedtime counting book.

The Happy Hocky Family by Lane Smith
Seventeen very short (and very funny) stories about a stick figure family provides fun for all ages.

I Love You Because You're You by Liz Baker
In rhyme, a mother describes her love for her child no matter what he does.

A Mother for Choco by Keiko Kasza
A lonely bird named Choco finds a mother who holds him, kisses him, and cheers him up.

The Very Best Daddy of All by Marion Dane Bauer and Leslie Wu
Pictures and rhyming text show how some fathers—animal, bird, and human—take care of their children.

Yesterday I Had the Blues by Jeron Ashford Frame
A young boy uses colors to capture a range of emotions, from "down in my shoes blues" to the kind of greens that "make you want to be Somebody." [featured on a *Between the Lions* episode]

Vocabulary

away	home
between	lonely
connect	mommy
feel	safe
feelings	scared
happy	trip

Materials

I Miss You, Stinky Face by Lisa McCourt and Cyd Moore
Owl Babies by Martin Waddell and Patrick Benson

Bunny Cakes

Skill Focus
Environmental Print
Story Comprehension
Story Elements (Characters)
Vocabulary

Theme Connections
Food

Vocabulary

cooking	ingredients
cooled	list
excited	measuring
frosting	cup
frustrated	mixing bowl
grocer	spoon
icing	thrilled

Materials

Bunny Cakes by Rosemary Wells

What to Do

- Read aloud *Bunny Cakes* to individuals or small groups.
- Point to the ingredients and the cooking tools and ask the children to name them.
- When Max drops the eggs, spills the milk, and knocks over the flour, point to the illustrations and ask the children to say what happened. Then point to Ruby's grocery list and ask, *What word did Ruby write on the list? What does she want Max to buy at the store?*
- When Max draws a picture of Red-Hot Marshmallow Squirters, ask the children to compare his drawing with the label on the box of Red-Hot Marshmallow Squirters on the next page.
- Talk with the children about how Max, Ruby, and Grandma feel.

Extension Idea

After reading the book, encourage the children to create shopping lists to make Red-Hot Marshmallow Squirters or another food, real or imaginary.

Click on the
*Between the
Lions* website!
pbskids.org/lions/gryphonhouse

Stories:
- Bee-bim Bop!
- Making Bread
- Stone Soup

Skill Focus

Concepts of Print
Making Connections
Vocabulary

Theme Connections

Food
Families

Too Many Tamales

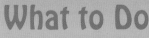

What to Do

▣ Read aloud *Too Many Tamales* to individuals or small groups.

▣ As you read the book, pause to encourage the children to make connections between the story events and their lives. Ask, *Have you ever helped your family make a special meal? What did you make? How did you help? Have you ever done something your mother or father told you not to do? What did you do? What happened?*

▣ Use the illustrations, gestures, and hand motions to explain the meaning of unfamiliar words and phrases such as *dusk, glittered, tamales,* masa *(dough), kneaded, sparkled, sparkling, pumping, disappeared, reappeared, folding, husk, steam, shock, littered, interrupt, confess,* niña *(girl),* and *groan.*

▣ At the end, invite the children to let out a groan "the size of twenty-four tamales"!

Extension Idea

Make tamales or another tasty treat with the children and serve the treat for snack.

Vocabulary

confess	masa (dough)
disappeared	niña (girl)
dusk	pumping
folding	reappeared
glittered	shock
groan	sparkled
husk	sparkling
interrupt	steam
kneaded	tamales
littered	

Material

Too Many Tamales by Gary Soto

Click on the *Between the Lions* website!
pbskids.org/lions/gryphonhouse

Stories:

▣ Bee-bim Bop!

▣ Cheesybreadville

▣ Making Bread

▣ Stone Soup

Three Books About Friends

Skill Focus
Social and Emotional Awareness
Story Comprehension
Vocabulary

Theme Connections
Friends
Feelings

Vocabulary

buddy	fun
cheer	happy
connect	help
friend	together

Materials

A Letter to Amy by
  Ezra Jack Keats
My Friends by Taro Gomi
Yo! Yes? by Chris Raschka

Click on the
*Between the
Lions* **website!**
pbskids.org/lions/gryphonhouse

Stories:
▨ Owen and Mzee
▨ Yo! Yes?

What to Do

▨ Read *A Letter to Amy*, *Yo! Yes?* and *My Friends* to the children.
▨ Help the children connect the stories to their experiences with friends. Talk about being a friend and having friends. For example:

  ▣ Ask, *What are some of the things we have learned about friends? What are some things that good friends do?*
  ▣ Ask, *What do like to do with your classroom buddy?* (See page 17.) *Who can tell me one thing that you and your buddy like to do together?*

▨ Sing "Yo! Yes! Do Your Best!" or "Make New Friends."

Yo! Yes! Do Your Best!
(*Tune: "This Old Man"*)
This good friend,
She said one. (*Hold up one finger.*)
She said "Come, let's have some fun."
With a Yo! Yes! Do your best,
Give a friend a cheer.
We are happy you are here.

This good friend,
He said two. (*Hold up two fingers.*)
He said, "Can I play with you?"
With a Yo! Yes! Do your best,
Give a friend a cheer.
We are happy you are here.

This good friend,
She said three. (*Hold up three fingers.*)
She said, "Will you play with me?"
With a Yo! Yes! Do your best,
Give a friend a cheer.
We are happy you are here.

This good friend,
He said four. (*Hold up four fingers.*)
He said, "Can we play some more?"
With a Yo! Yes! Do your best,
Give a friend a cheer.
We are happy you are here.
Hip! Hip! Hooray! (*Children cheer.*)

Make New Friends
(*Tune: Traditional*)
Make new friends,
But keep the old.
One is silver,
The other is gold.

A circle is round,
It has no end.
That's how long,
I will be your friend.

You have one hand,
I have the other.
Put them together, (*Children hold hands.*)
We have each other.

Cleo and Theo's Book Suggestions

Being Friends
by Karen Beaumont
Despite their differences, two girls know that the key to friendship is having one special thing in common: they like being friends.

Earl's Too Cool for Me by Leah Komaiko and Laura Cornell
Even though Earl is so cool that he "taught an octopus how to scrub," he's willing to make new friends. [featured on a *Between the Lions* episode]

How to Lose All Your Friends by Nancy Carlson
This book tells what to do to make sure that you don't have any friends. In the process, children learn positive behaviors that help them make and get along with friends.

Lissy's Friends by Grace Lin
Lissy is lonely on her first day of school, so she makes a bird from origami paper to keep her company. Soon she has a group of folded animal friends. When they blow away, a new friend comes to the rescue.

When I Was Five
by Arthur Howard
A six-year-old boy remembers all the things he loved when he was five. Many of his favorite things have changed, except for his best friend. [featured on a *Between the Lions* episode]

Will I Have a Friend?
by Miriam Cohen
Jim is nervous on his first day of school. He doesn't know anyone, and doesn't know if he will find anyone to be his friend.

Two Stories About Helping

Skill Focus
Letter Recognition
Making Connections
Phonological Awareness
(Beginning Sounds)
Vocabulary

Theme Connection
Helping

Vocabulary

big	lion
classroom	little
connect	mouse
enormous	small
grateful	thankful
help	

Materials

alphabet chart

The Enormous Potato by Aubrey Davis and Dusan Petricic

The Lion and the Mouse by Bernadette Watts

Click on the *Between the Lions* website!
pbskids.org/lions/gryphonhouse

Stories:

- ◫ Just What Mama Needs
- ◫ The Lion and the Mouse
- ◫ The Little Red Hen

What to Do

- ◫ Read the books *The Lion and the Mouse* and *The Enormous Potato* to the children.
- ◫ Ask questions to help the children make connections between their lives and the topics in the books. For example:
  - ◫ Say, *Tell me one way you help in our classroom.*
  - ◫ Say, *Name some things that are enormous. Name some things that are little.*
  - ◫ Say, *Look at this word. It's the word* little. *Who can show me the letter "l" in the word* little? *Who can find the letter "Ll" on our alphabet chart?*
  - ◫ Invite the children to join you in reading the class story (see page 89).

Cleo and Theo's Book Suggestions

Cucumber Soup by Vickie Leigh Krudwig and Craig McFarland Brown
Ten black ants and a tiny flea move a cucumber.

The Enormous Turnip by Aleksei Tolstoy and Scott Goto
This is a retelling of the classic tale for young readers.

The Giant Carrot by Jan Peck and Barry Root
The Russian folktale is retold as a Texas yarn.

The Gigantic Turnip by Aleksei Tolstoy and Niamh Sharkey
Only when a tiny mouse joins in can a group uproot this giant vegetable.

Grandma Lena's Big Ol' Turnip
by Denia Lewis Hester and Jackie Urbanovic
This retelling of ***The Gigantic Turnip*** is about teamwork, sharing, and cooking in an extended African American family.

How Chipmunk Got His Stripes
by Joseph and James Bruchac, Jose Aruego, and Ariane Dewey
In this Native American tale, a little squirrel challenges a big bear and is transformed into a chipmunk.

Skill Focus
Making Connections
Phonological Awareness
(Beginning Sounds, Ending
Sounds)

Theme Connections
Nighttime
Sounds

"Night Music"

What to Do
☒ Engage the children in a discussion about nighttime.
☒ Ask, *What are some of the sounds you hear at night before you go to sleep?*
☒ Recite "Night Music" together.

Night Music
Night in the country,
Listen to the sounds.
Night in the country,
There are noises all around.

Listen to the wind,
Whispering through the trees.
Listen to the frogs,
Chanting in the breeze.

Night in the country,
Listen to the sounds.
Night in the country,
There's music all around.

☒ Say, *Some animals are active at night.* Ask, *What is a bird that hunts for food at night and sleeps during the day?* (an owl)
☒ Say, *I'm thinking of an animal that is active at night. It looks like it is wearing a mask. It has rings on its tail. Its name begins with an "Rr" /r/. What is it?* (a raccoon)
☒ Say, *I'm going to say some words. If the word begins with the /n/ sound, touch your nose. Say the following words: night, noise, two, napkin,* and *moon. After each word, ask, Did you hear the /n/ sound at the beginning of the word? If you did, touch your nose.*

Vocabulary

chant	nighttime
country	sounds
frog	tree
listen	whisper
music	wind
night	

Materials

none needed

Click on the
*Between the
Lions* website!
pbskids.org/lions/gryphonhouse

Stories:
☒ Night in the Country
☒ Night Shift

Good Night, Gorilla

Skill Focus
Concepts of Print
Interpreting Illustrations
Storytelling
Vocabulary

Theme Connection
Nighttime

Vocabulary

armadillo	lion
elephant	lock
flashlight	open
giraffe	unlock
gorilla	watchman
hyena	zoo
key	zookeeper

Material

Good Night, Gorilla by Peggy Rathmann

What to Do

- Explore the book *Good Night, Gorilla* with individuals or small groups.
- Construct the story together by examining and discussing the pictures.
- Ask questions such as, *What is the gorilla doing? What color is his cage? What color key does he use to open the cage? What do you see inside the (elephant's) cage? What is the mouse doing?*
- Point out the words inside the speech bubbles and invite the children to "read" the predictable words with you.
- Talk about the scenes in the dark, after the zookeeper turns off the light. *Who is saying goodnight?* Match the eyes in the dark with the eyes of the zookeeper's wife on the next page.

Extension Idea

Encourage the children to draw and write or dictate their own bedtime stories, real or imagined.

Skill Focus

Dictating Sentences
Parts of a Book
Sequencing
Story Structure
Storytelling

Theme Connection

Stories

Make a Book

AGE
3+

What to Do

- Have the children make their own books by folding a piece of paper in half.
- The first page will be the front cover of the book. Have the children draw their stories on the second, third, and fourth pages.
- Ask questions to help the children name the characters in their stories and to sequence the story events. *Who is in your story? What happens first? What happens next? How does your story end?* The stories can be wordless, or you can write the story on the pages as the children dictate them to you.
- Have the children give their story a title. Help the children write the titles and their first and last names on the cover.
- Invite the children to share their books with the class.

Extension Idea

Display the books in the Library Center for the children to read to one another.

Vocabulary

author	illustrator
end	next
first	title
front cover	

Materials

crayons

markers

paper

pencils

Radio Station

Skill Focus
Asking Questions
Imaginative Play
Listening and Speaking
Story Comprehension
Vocabulary

Theme Connection
Stories

Vocabulary

broadcast   news
interview   radio station
microphone

Materials

paper and markers (to create
     the a radio station sign)
pretend microphone (made
     from a paper towel tube that
     is cut in half and an
     aluminum foil ball)
writing materials (clipboards,
     notepads, pencils, markers)

What to Do

- Help the children create a radio station sign (for example, Children's Public Radio).
- Talk about what happens at a radio station, including what happens during an interview. *When you interview someone, you ask that person questions about things you and other people want to know.*
- Have the children take turns interviewing one another and different storybook characters for the "radio station."
- Brainstorm different storybook characters the children can interview, such as the farmer in *The Enormous Potato*, the cows or the ducks in *Click, Clack, Moo*, or the wolf in "The Three Little Pigs."
- This is a fun, creative way for children to retell stories.

Extension Idea

Place the radio station sign and pretend microphone in the Pretend and Play Center for the children to use independently.

Skill Focus

Concepts of Print
Story Structure
Storytelling
Vocabulary

Theme Connection
Stories

Our Own Potato Story

What to Do

- Read *The Enormous Potato*, a version of the Russian folktale called *The Giant Turnip*, to the children.
- Suggest that the class write and illustrate a version of the folktale or create a folktale about another enormous vegetable that children are familiar with, such as a carrot or a sweet potato.
- Brainstorm a fruit or vegetable that the characters will pull out of the ground. Then brainstorm the people and animals that will try to pull the fruit or vegetable out of the ground. Prompt children to think of animals from their environment, such as deer, foxes, opossums, armadillos, and weasels.
- Have the class put the characters in order from biggest to littlest.
- Ask questions to help the children write the story. *Who does the farmer call to help him pull the sweet potato out of the ground? Who will pull next? Will the sweet potato come out of the ground now? What will our characters do with the sweet potato when it comes out of the ground?*
- Begin writing the story on sheets of chart paper. Continue for as long as the children remain interested. If their interest wanes, tell them that you will continue writing the story another day.

Vocabulary

bigger	gigantic
biggest	huge
characters	littlest
enormous	order
folktale	potato
giant	story

Material

chart paper
The Enormous Potato by Aubrey Davis and Dusan Petricic
markers

Extension Idea

Help the class come up with a title for the story. Together, brainstorm different words for *enormous* such as *giant, gigantic, huge, mammoth,* and *gargantuan,* and choose one for the title. Read the completed story to the children, pointing to each word as you read. Invite the children to join in the telling.

Click on the *Between the Lions* website!
pbskids.org/lions/gryphonhouse

Song: My Favorite Word (humongous)

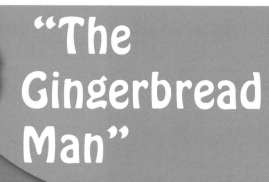

"The Gingerbread Man"

Skill Focus

Listening and Speaking
Phonological Awareness
Story Comprehension

Theme Connections

Traditional Tales/Stories
Animals

Vocabulary

bear
cookie
farmer
fox
gingerbread
imagine
refrain

retell
run away
story
version
wolf
words

Materials

chart paper
markers

Click on the
*Between the
Lions* website!
pbskids.org/lions/gryphonhouse

Story: Stop That Pickle!

Preparation

▣ Write the refrain from the story on chart paper.

What to Do

▣ Instead of reading a book that tells the story of "The Gingerbread Man," tell the children your version. Have fun mixing in story figures from other tales. For example, instead of running away from three farmers, a bear, a wolf, and a fox, the gingerbread man in your story might run away from a giraffe, a gorilla, and a lion.

▣ Tell the children that you are going to tell them a story about a little cookie that runs away. Ask if anyone has every heard the story of "The Gingerbread Man."

▣ Tell the children that you would like them to help you tell the story. Write the refrain from the story on chart paper. Point to the words as you read the refrain:

> Run, run,
> As fast as you can.
> You can't catch me
> I'm the gingerbread man.

▣ Invite the children to join in as you chant and point to the words.

▣ Now you are ready to tell the story. Explain that one of the nice things about telling a story is that each storyteller can tell it in a different way. Introduce the characters in your version of the tale. Then tell the story.

▣ Try to change your voice and mannerism for each new character the gingerbread man meets.

▣ Invite the children to chime in each time the gingerbread man chants, "Run, run, as fast as you can.…"

Skill Focus
Concepts of Print
Sequencing
Storytelling

Theme Connection
Traditional Tales/Stories
Food

Our Gingerbread Man Story Map

AGE 4+

What to Do

- Tell the children that together you will be writing a version of "The Gingerbread Man." Say, *What if we made a gingerbread man and he ran away from our classroom? Where would he go? Who would he meet? What would happen to the gingerbread man at the end of our story?*

- Let the children come up with story ideas in response to your questions. Write down their ideas. Tell the children that instead of writing a book, you are going to make a story map to tell the story.

- Draw a simple house shape and then cut it out. Put it on the left side of a bulletin board. If you have a class photo, glue it in the house. Say, *This is our school. This is where we baked the gingerbread man.* Draw a paper path across the board. Say, *This is where the gingerbread man ran.*

- Ask, *Who is the first person (or animal) our gingerbread man meets?* Write the name on a label and put it on the board. Draw a simple picture of that person (or animal).

- Ask, *What does that person (or animal) say to the gingerbread man?* Write the words the children provide in a piece of paper cut in the shape of a speech bubble. Attach it to the bulletin board.

- Ask, *What does the gingerbread man say?* Write the children's words in another speech bubble and attach it to the bulletin board.

- Repeat this process until the gingerbread man has met three to four people and the story has ended.

- Invite a child to move a gingerbread man cookie or paper cutout along the path. Narrate the story, encouraging the children to join in.

Vocabulary

bulletin board	speech bubble
first person	story
gingerbread man	story map
	together
house	version
label	write

Materials

bulletin board
class photo (optional)
glue or tape
labels
markers
paper
scissors

Click on the *Between the Lions* website!
pbskids.org/lions/gryphonhouse

Story: Stop That Pickle!

Chapter 5

Learning Phonological and Phonemic Awareness

The activities in this chapter of *Wild About Literacy* focus on learning, singing, and talking about words and their sounds as a fun way to help children learn phonological and phonemic awareness (see The Literacy Scope and Sequence on pages 14–15). The following activities help children learn and play with the sounds of spoken language, and also help children build a solid foundation in phonological awareness, which children need before they begin to learn phonics.

Hint: If you do not know the tunes mentioned in the activities, use one of the many websites to find the song or a CD that features the song. Some possibilities include songsforteaching.com, kididdles.com, amazon.com, and itunes.com.

The activities in this chapter are grouped alphabetically by topic (or theme) and then by age (3+ or 4+) within each topic. The activities have the following components:

Skill Focus	Materials
Theme Connection(s)	Preparation (if necessary)
Vocabulary	What to Do

Skill Focus—lists the literacy skills that the activity addresses and other skills that young children need to learn, such as fine motor skills or emotional awareness.

Theme Connections—lists one or two familiar early childhood themes that the activity covers. If more than one theme is listed, the first is the one with the strongest connection.

Vocabulary—lists words that are part of the activity. Use these when you are engaging children in the activity, defining their

A Note About Repetition: You will find the same songs, poems, and books used in multiple activities in *Wild About Literacy*. Children benefit and learn from repetition. When children hear a familiar song or poem, they may learn something new or solidify what they already know. Using a familiar song or story to teach a new skill is a technique used by many teachers, which is why you will find repetition in this book.

meaning if necessary. Repeat these words throughout the day so children hear the words used in context and can begin to understand how each word is used.

Materials—lists, in alphabetical order, the materials you will need to do the activity. Be sure you have the materials you need before you begin the activity.

Preparation—If the activity needs any preparation, such as writing a song or poem on chart paper or preparing a chart, what you need to do is described in this section.

What to Do—Step by step, this section outlines how to engage children in the activity.

In addition, many activities include ideas that build on the main activity, extend it to another curriculum area, or suggest books that relate to the activity.

Many children's books are suggested as a way to extend one or more activities in this chapter. Some of the book suggestions in this chapter include:

All Kinds of Clothes by Jeri S. Cipriano

City Lullaby by Marilyn Singer and Carll Cneut

The Colors of Us by Karen Katz

Harold and the Purple Crayon by Crockett Johnson

Hats Hats Hats by Ann Morris and Ken Heyman

Lily Brown's Paintings by Angela Johnson and E. B. Lewis

The Listening Walk by Paul Showers and Aliki

My Colors, My World/Mis Colores, Mi Mundo
   by Maya Christina Gonzalez

New Clothes for New Year's Day by Hyun-joo Bae

New Shoes for Sylvia by Johanna Hurwitz

Red Is a Dragon: A Book of Colors
   by Roseanne Thong and Grace Lin

Sounds All Around by Wendy Pfeffer and Holly Keller

Sounds of the Wild: Nighttime by Maurice Pledger

Suki's Kimono by Chieri Uegaki and Stephanie Jorisch

Two Pair of Shoes by Esther Sanderson

Yellow Elephant: A Bright Bestiary
   by Julie Larios and Julie Paschkis

Click on the
*Between the
Lions* website!
pbskids.org/lions/gryphonhouse

Books About Reading
Books Featured on *Between the Lions*
Recommended Books

Skill Focus

Phonological Awareness
(Clapping Syllables in Names;
Rhythm, Rhyme, and
Repetition)

Theme Connections

All About Me
Friends

"Hello, Hello, Everyone"

What to Do

- Have the children sit in a circle.
- Sing "Hello, Hello, Everyone."

    Hello, Hello, Everyone
    (*Tune: "Twinkle, Twinkle, Little Star"*)
    Hello, hello, everyone,
    Let's clap our names
    And have some fun.
    Say your name
    And clap along.
    It will sound just like a song.
    Hello, hello, everyone,
    Let's clap our names
    And have some fun.

- Then say, *Let's go around the circle and clap everyone's names.*
    Start by saying your name slowly in its natural rhythm, then
    repeat your name and clap as you say each word part:

Ms.	Pe	ter	son
clap	clap	clap	clap

- Ask the child sitting to your left to say his name. Then repeat
    the name as you clap each syllable or part. Ask the children to
    clap with you.
- Continue around the circle until you have clapped each child's
    name. Don't worry if this is difficult at first. Practice will help
    the children hear the syllables and clap along.
- Sing "Hello, Hello, Everyone" again.

Vocabulary

circle   hello
clap   song
everybody   sound
fun

Materials

none needed

"Hickety Pickety Bumblebee"

Skill Focus

Phonological Awareness
(Clapping Syllables in Names;
Stomping Syllables in Names;
Rhythm, Rhyme, and Repetition)

Theme Connections

All About Me

Opposites

Vocabulary

beats	name
bumblebee	opposites
fast	quiet
hello	slow
loud	

Materials

toy or paper bumblebee

Click on the
*Between the
Lions* website!
pbskids.org/lions/gryphonhouse

Video Clips:

▣ Opposite Bunny: fast/slow

▣ Opposite Bunny: loud/quiet

Game: Hopposites

What to Do

▣ Have the children sit in a circle.

▣ Hold up a stuffed toy or paper bumblebee. Say, *This is our bumblebee, Hickety Pickety. Let's all say hello to him.*

▣ Chant the first verse of "Hickety Pickety Bumblebee."

> **Hickety Pickety Bumblebee**
> Hickety Pickety Bumblebee
> Won't you say your name for me? (*Point to a child; signal child to say name.*)

▣ Signal the child to your left to say her name.

▣ Chant the second verse. Repeat for each child.

> Let's all say it fast! (*All say child's name quickly.*)
> Let's all say it slow! (*All say child's name slowly.*)

▣ On the same day or another day, say, *When we chanted "Hickety Pickety Bumblebee," we said everyone's names fast and slow. Fast and slow are opposites. This time we are going to do two more opposites:* loud *and* quiet. *Let me hear you say "hello" in a big, loud voice. Now let me hear you say "hello" in a little, quiet voice.*

▣ Chant the first and third verses of "Hickety Pickety Bumblebee" for each child.

> Let's all say it loudly. (*All shout child's name.*)
> Let's all say it quietly. (*All whisper child's name.*)

On the same day or another day, chant the first and fourth verses of "Hickety Pickety Bumblebee." This time, clap the beats in each child's name.

> Hickety Pickety Bumblebee
> Won't you say your name for me? (*Point to a child; signal child to say name.*)

Let's all clap the beats. (*All clap beats in child's name.*)

On the same day or another day, chant the first and fifth verses of "Hickety Pickety Bumblebee." This time you will stomp the beats in each child's name.

> Hickety Pickety Bumblebee
> Won't you say your name for me? (*Point to a child; signal child to say name.*)

Let's all stomp the beats! (*All stomp the beats in the name.*)

Chant the first, second, and fourth verses of "Hickety Pickety Bumblebee," and then challenge the children to make up verses.

Cleo and Theo's Book Suggestions

Catalina Magdalena Hoopensteiner Wallendiner Hogan Logan Bogan Was Her Name by Tedd Arnold
The author transforms a traditional camp song into a wild, wacky book about a deliriously happy young girl with an unusually long name.

A Mother for Choco by Keiko Kasza
A lonely bird named Choco finds a mother who holds him, kisses him, and cheers him up.

AGE
3+ "Dress, Dress, Dress Yourself"

Skill Focus
Phonological Awareness
(Rhythm, Rhyme, and Repetition)
Vocabulary

Theme Connections
All About Me
Clothing
Sounds

Vocabulary

buckle	learn
button	practice
day	snap
dress	Velcro
fastener	yourself
hook	zipper
hook-and-	
loop	

Materials

clothing with different kinds of fasteners (buttons, zippers, snaps, hooks, buckles, and hook-and-loop)

What to Do

▣ Before singing the song, show the children clothing with different kinds of fasteners (buttons, zippers, snaps, hooks, buckles, and hook-and-loop).

▣ Demonstrate how each fastener works.

▣ Let the children practice opening and closing the fasteners. Emphasize that some fasteners are hard to use, but with practice and patience they will learn—they will be able to get dressed all by themselves!

▣ Teach the children "Dress, Dress, Dress Yourself."

> **Dress, Dress, Dress Yourself**
> (*Tune: "Row, Row, Row Your Boat"*)
> Dress, dress, dress yourself
> Every single day.
> Snappity, snappity, snappity, snappity
> So that you can play.

▣ Repeat the song, telling the children to raise their hand each time they hear the /s/ sound. Repeat the song again, drawing out the /ssssss/ sounds in the song.

Extension Idea

Put the clothing in the Pretend and Play Center so the children can continue practicing opening a closing fasteners.

Click on the *Between the Lions* website!
pbskids.org/lions/gryphonhouse

Video Clips:
▣ Fred Says (zipper)
▣ un People: buttoned/unbuttoned

Skill Focus
Fine Motor Skills
Phonological Awareness
(Rhythm, Rhyme, and
Repetition)

Theme Connection
Animals

"The Itsy-Bitsy Spider"

What to Do

▣ Tell the children that songs can tell stories. Say, *Listen as I sing you a story about a very small animal. The title of the song is "The Itsy-Bitsy Spider."* Itsy-bitsy *means "very small or tiny."*

▣ Show the children how to use the thumb and pointing finger of each hand to make the itsy-bitsy spider climb through the air, or just have the fingers on one hand climb up your arm.

▣ Sing the song with the children, adding hand motions.

The Itsy-Bitsy Spider
(Tune: Traditional)
The itsy-bitsy spider
Climbed up the waterspout.
Down came the rain
And washed the spider out.
Up came the sun
And dried out all the rain.
And the itsy-bitsy spider
Climbed up the spout again.

▣ As you sing the song again, tell the children to listen for the words that rhyme (waterspout/out, rain/again).

Vocabulary

again	spider
animal	story
climb	sun
down	thumb
finger	tiny
itsy-bitsy	up
rain	very small
small	waterspout
song	

Materials

none needed

"Elephants Walk"

Skill Focus

Phonological Awareness (Rhythm and Rhyme)
Vocabulary

Theme Connections

Animals
Opposites
Rhymes

Vocabulary

big	left
elephant	right
foot	slow
four	trunk
gray	walk

Materials

none needed

What to Do

- Have the children stand and raise their right foot and then their left foot.
- Recite the poem "Elephants Walk."

  Elephants Walk
  Right foot, left foot, see me go.
  I am gray and big and slow.
  I come walking down the street,
  With my trunk and four big feet.

- As you read the poem again, pause before each rhyming word ("slow" in line two and "feet" in line four), and ask the children to say the rhyming word.
- Form a circle with the children.
- Clasp your hands and pretend your arms are your trunk. Together walk slowly and heavily, swinging your "trunks" as you chant the rhyme together.

Extension Idea

Write the poem on chart paper and ask the children to find the letter "T" everywhere in the poem.

Click on the
*Between the
Lions* website!
pbskids.org/lions/gryphonhouse

Song: Monkey Match (rhymes)

"Mary Wore Her Red Dress"

Skill Focus
Color Identification
Phonological Awareness (Rhythm and Repetition)
Vocabulary

Theme Connections
Colors
Clothing

What to Do

▣ Have the children sit in a circle.
▣ Teach them "Mary Wore Her Red Dress."

> **Mary Wore Her Red Dress**
> Mary wore her red dress, red dress, red dress.
> Mary wore her red dress all day long.

▣ Create a verse for each child. Ask the child sitting next to you to name something he is wearing. For example, ask, *What color are your (sneakers)?* Sing:

> Henry wore his black sneakers, black sneakers,
>   black sneakers.
> Henry wore his black sneakers all day long.

▣ Repeat the process until you have sung a verse for each child.

Cleo and Theo's Book Suggestions

The Colors of Us by Karen Katz
   A young girl mixes colors to paint pictures of her family and friends in all their different shades.

My Colors, My World/Mis Colores, Mi Mundo
   by Maya Christina Gonzalez
   A girl living in the desert describes the colors that remind her of the people and places she loves.

Red Is a Dragon by Roseanne Thong and Grace Lin
   The colors that surround a young Chinese American girl remind her of the things that she loves.

Vocabulary

all day long	dress
black	red
circle	sneakers
color	wore

Materials

none needed

Click on the
*Between the
Lions* website!
pbskids.org/lions/gryphonhouse

Stories:
▣ POP POP POP POP POP
▣ Spicy Hot Colors
▣ Yesterday I Had the Blues

"Miss Mary Mack"

Skill Focus

Phonological Awareness (Rhyme, Rhythm, and Repetition)
Hand-Eye Coordination
Vocabulary

Theme Connections

Colors
Clothing

Vocabulary

back	pockets
black	purple
buttons	red
dressed	ribbons
green	rosy
jeans	silver

Materials

none needed

Click on the
*Between the
Lions* website!
pbskids.org/lions/gryphonhouse

Stories:
- POP POP POP POP POP
- Spicy Hot Colors
- Yesterday I Had the Blues

Poem: Yellow
Video Clip: Colorful Foods

What to Do

- Ask the children, *Do you have a favorite color you like to wear?*
- Tell them you are going to teach them a song about a girl named Mary who likes to wear black.
- Sing "Miss Mary Mack" without the motions.

   Miss Mary Mack
   Miss Mary Mack, Mack, Mack (*Clap hands together on each beat.*)
   All dressed in black, black, black, (*Clap hands against partner's on each beat.*)
   With silver buttons, buttons, buttons (*Clap hands together on each beat.*)
   All down her back, back, back. (*Clap hands against partner's on each beat.*)

   Additional verses:
   Miss Mary Sted, Sted, Sted
   All dressed in red, red, red,
   With rosy ribbons, ribbons, ribbons
   All over her head, head, head.

   Miss Mary Bean, Bean, Bean
   All dressed in green, green, green,
   With purple pockets, pockets, pockets
   All down her jeans, jeans, jeans.

- Once the children have learned the words, teach them the hand-clapping pattern.
- Challenge the children to make up new verses with other colors.

Skill Focus
Gross Motor Development
Phonological Awareness
(Rhythm, Rhyme, and
Repetition)
Vocabulary

Theme Connection
Colors

"Rainbow Song"

What to Do

- Draw a rainbow on a piece of paper using red, orange, yellow, green, blue, and purple markers or crayons. Ask, *Does anyone know what this is called? Has anyone ever seen a rainbow? Where did you see it?*

- Explain that we can sometimes see a rainbow in the sky if the sun comes out right after it rains.

- Have the children name the colors of the rainbow as you point to them. Then sing the "Rainbow Song" with the children.

Rainbow Song
(Tune: "Twinkle, Twinkle, Little Star")
Red and orange,
Green and blue,
Sunny yellow, purple too.
All the colors that we know
Paint the sky in a rainbow.
Red and orange,
Green and blue,
Sunny yellow, purple, too.

- Sing the song again, pausing before the end of the third, fifth, and eighth lines. Ask the children to say the rhyming word.

Extension Idea

Have six children stand in front of the class each with a ribbon or crepe paper streamer in one of the six rainbow colors. The children can make their streamers dance by moving their arms up and down or side to side or in figure eights as the class sings the "Rainbow Song" together.

Vocabulary

blue	rainbow
green	red
orange	sky
purple	yellow
rain	

Materials

paper
red, orange, yellow, green, blue, and purple markers or crayons

Click on the *Between the Lions* website!
pbskids.org/lions/gryphonhouse

Stories:
- POP POP POP POP POP
- Spicy Hot Colors
- Yesterday I Had the Blues
Poem: Yellow
Video Clip: Colorful Foods

Color Rhymes

Skill Focus
Color Recognition
Phonological Awareness
(Rhyming)

Theme Connections
Colors
Rhymes

Vocabulary

bean   red
bed   rhyme
blue   shoe
green   sink
kite   white
pink

Materials

pictures (or picture cards) of the
    following: bed, (green) bean,
    kite, sink, and shoe
red, green, white, pink, and
    blue crayons

What to Do

- Invite the children to play a rhyming game.
- Have the children repeat these words after you: *red, head, said, Fred*. Ask, *What do you notice? Yes, these words all rhyme!*
- Place a red, green, white, pink, and blue crayon on the table along with pictures (or picture cards) of the following: bed, (green) bean, kite, sink, and shoe. Point to and name the pictures with the children.
- Hold up a red crayon and ask, *Can you find a picture that rhymes with red? Yes,* red *and* bed *are two words that rhyme.* Have the children repeat the words *red* and *bed* with you. Place the red crayon and the picture of the bed off to one side.
- Repeat these steps with the blue, green, white, and pink crayons.

Cleo and Theo's Book Suggestions

My Colors, My World/Mis Colores, Mi Mundo
by Maya Christina Gonzalez
A girl living in the desert describes the colors that remind her of the people and places she loves.

Spicy Hot Colors: Colores Picantes by Sherry Shahan
Colors explode off the page in this energetic, jazzy picture book introducing readers to colors in English and Spanish. [featured on a *Between the Lions* episode]

Yellow Elephant: A Bright Bestiary
by Julie Larios and Julie Paschkis
Rhyming poems describe a variety of colorful animals.

Yesterday I Had the Blues
by Jeron Ashford Frame
A young boy uses colors to capture a range of emotions, from "down in my shoes blues" to the kind of greens that "make you want to be Somebody." [featured on a *Between the Lions* episode]

Click on the
*Between the
Lions* website!
pbskids.org/lions/gryphonhouse

Story: Spicy Hot Colors
Poem: Yellow
Game: Monkey Match (rhymes)

Skill Focus
Counting
Phonological Awareness (Rhythm and Rhyme)

Theme Connection
Counting

"One, Two, Buckle My Shoe"

What to Do

☐ Teach the children "One, Two, Buckle My Shoe."

One, Two, Buckle My Shoe
One, two,
Buckle my shoe.
Three, four,
Shut the door.
Five, six,
Pick up sticks.
Seven, eight,
Lay them straight.
Nine, ten,
A big fat hen.
Let's get up and count again.

☐ Ask the children to listen for the rhyming words (two/shoe, four/door, six/sticks, eight/straight, ten/hen) as you say the rhyme together. Do the children notice the rhyming pattern?

Extension Idea

Ask the children who have laces on their shoes to stand. Then ask the children who have Velcro on their shoes to stand. Continue the process with the children who have buckles, zippers, and buttons on their shoes. Finally, ask the children who have slip-on shoes to stand. Make a chart showing the different kinds of shoes the children have. Have the children write their name under the column that matches the type of shoe they are wearing.

Vocabulary

again	one
buckle	save
button	shoe
count	shoelace
door	six
eight	stick
fat	straight
five	ten
four	three
hen	two
laces	Velcro
nine	zipper

Materials

none needed

AGE **4+**

Count the Words

Skill Focus
Phonological Awareness
(Counting Words in a
Sentence)

Theme Connection
Counting

Vocabulary

class book   sentence
count   slowly
cube   word
read

Materials

unifix cubes or blocks

What to Do

▣ Give each child a set of five small cubes or blocks. Tell the children you are going to read them some sentences from the "I Can" class book (see page 186).

▣ Say, *Every time you hear a word, put down one cube.* Demonstrate as you say, *Just…like…this.*

▣ Choose a three-word sentence from the class book. Point to the sentence as you read it slowly. Say, *This is a sentence.* Point to each word and say, *These are words. A sentence is made up of words.*

▣ Say the sentence again. As you say each word, pick up a cube or block and put it in front of you, from left to right. Have the children do the same with their cubes or blocks. At the end of the sentence, everyone should have a row of three cubes or blocks.

▣ Ask, *How many words in the sentence,* I can (swim)? (Touch a cube or block as you say each word.) *Yes, three words.*

▣ Repeat this process with several other three-to-five-word sentences.

Extension Idea

Say, *I am going to say the names of two animals. Listen carefully, then tell me which word is longer.* Slowly say the following pairs of words: *cow/armadillo, dog/giraffe, pig/gorilla, lion/elephant.* After the children have answered, show them each word pair in print, with one word written directly below the other, to see if their answers were correct.

Skill Focus
Active Listening
Phonological Awareness
(Clapping and Counting
Syllables)

Theme Connections
Counting
Clothing

Clapping and Counting Syllables

Preparation
☒ Place clothes items into a bag.
☒ Label three boxes with the numbers 1, 2, and 3.

What to Do
☒ Ask a volunteer to pull out a piece of clothing and name it. Then repeat the word (*neck-tie*) as you clap the syllables or word parts.
☒ Have the children put the clothing with one syllable in the 1 box, the clothing with two syllables in the 2 box, and so on.
☒ After all the clothes have been sorted, clap the names of the clothes in each box with the children.

Cleo and Theo's Book Suggestions
All Kinds of Clothes by Jeri S. Cipriano
This nonfiction book describes the clothing people wear to keep themselves warm or cool.

Hats Hats Hats by Ann Morris and Ken heyman
Learn about the many different hats worn around the world.

Joseph Had a Little Overcoat by Simms Taback
A very old overcoat is recycled numerous times into a variety of garments. [featured on a *Between the Lions* episode]

New Clothes for New Year's Day by Hyun-joo Bae
Follow the adventures of a young Korean girl as she prepares for the Lunar New Year.

New Shoes for Sylvia by Johanna Hurwitz
Sylvia receives a pair of beautiful red shoes from her Tia Rosita and finds ways to use them until she grows big enough for them to fit.

Two Pair of Shoes by Esther Sanderson
Maggie, a young Cree girl, receives two pairs of shoes for her birthday: black, patent-leather shoes and handmade beaded moccasins.

Vocabulary

box	parts
clap	sort
clothing	syllable
count	word

Materials

bag
items of clothing
markers
three boxes

"Where Is Mama?"

Skill Focus

Fine Motor Skills

Phonological Awareness (Rhythm and Repetition)

Vocabulary

Theme Connections

Families

Feelings

Vocabulary

bend	home
brother	left
daddy	mama
families	right
family	sing
feel	sister
finger	song
grandma	thumb
grandpa	today
happy	

Materials

none needed

What to Do

- Tell the children that they are going to use their fingers to sing a song about families.
- Before singing the song, put your hands behind your back. Then bring out your right thumb and bend it. Repeat with your left thumb. Tell the children that this finger is called a thumb.
- Have the children put their hands behind their backs. Then ask them to bring out their thumbs and bend them. Repeat with the other fingers.
- Sing and demonstrate the finger motions to this variation of "Where Is Thumbkin?" a few times before asking the children to join in.

> **Where Is Mama?**
> (*Tune: "Frère Jacques"*)
> Where is Mama? (*Hands behind back.*)
> Where is Mama?
> Here I am. (*Bring out right fist, and hold up right thumb.*)
> Here I am. (*Bring out left fist, and hold up left thumb.*)
> How do you feel today, Mama? (*Bend right thumb.*)
> Very happy, thank you. (*Bend left thumb.*)
> Let's go home. (*Bend right thumb downward and bring right hand behind back.*)
> Let's go home. (*Bend left thumb downward and bring left hand behind back.*)

- Repeat with daddy, brother, sister, grandma, and so on. Use a different finger for each new family member.

Extension Idea

Select five children (one for each finger and the thumb) to act out this song.

Skill Focus
Phonological Awareness (Rhyme)

Theme Connections
Families
Sounds

Rhyming Words

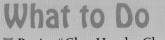
AGE 3+

What to Do

☑ Recite "Clap Hands, Clap Hands."

Clap Hands, Clap Hands
Clap hands, clap hands
'Til Mommy comes home.
She went on a plane
To visit Aunt Jane.

Clap hands, clap hands,
'Til Grandma comes home.
She went on a bus
To visit Grandpa Gus.

Clap hands, clap hands,
'Til Daddy comes home.
He went on a ship
To visit cousin Skip.
Have a nice trip! (*Wave goodbye.*)

▣ Point out some of the rhyming words in the song "Clap Hands, Clap Hands."

▣ Repeat the first verse of the song. Point out that the words *plane* and *Jane* rhyme. Say, *When words rhyme, they sound the same at the end. Plane and Jane sound the same at the end. It's fun to say rhyming words. Let's say the rhyming words together: plane, Jane.*

▣ Repeat for the words *bus* and *Gus* in the second verse.

▣ Repeat for the words *Skip, ship,* and *trip* in the third verse. Point out that the words rhyme because they end with /ip/.

Vocabulary

aunt	Jane
bus	plane
clap	rhyme
cousin	rhyming
daddy	same
end	ship
goodbye	Skip
grandma	sounds
grandpa	together
Gus	trip
hands	verse
home	wave

Materials

none needed

Click on the *Between the Lions* website!
pbskids.org/lions/gryphonhouse

Games:
▣ Dub Cubs
▣ Monkey Match (rhymes)

"I Eat My Peas"

Skill Focus

Active Listening
Phonological Awareness (Rhythm and Rhyme)
Vocabulary

Theme Connection

Food

Vocabulary

eat	peas
fork	poem
funny	recite
honey	rhyme
knife	spoon
life	taste
listen	words

Materials

none needed

What to Do

- Ask the children, *How do you eat peas? With a spoon? A fork? A knife? Your fingers?*
- Tell the children that you are going to recite a poem about eating peas. Ask them to listen carefully to the words to find out how the child in the poem eats peas.
- Recite "I Eat My Peas."

> **I Eat My Peas**
> I eat my peas with honey.
> I've done it all my life.
> It makes the peas taste funny.
> But it keeps them on the knife.

- Ask, *What does the child in the poem use to eat peas?*
- Recite the poem a second time, pausing to let the children supply the last rhyming word (*knife*). (Remind children to eat *their* peas with a fork or spoon.)

Cleo and Theo's Book Suggestions

Bee-bim Bop! by Linda Sue Park
In playful verse with a bouncy beat a young girl describes how her mom makes the popular Korean dish called Bee-bim bop. [featured on a *Between the Lions* episode]

Bread Is for Eating by David and Phillis Gershator
A mother sings a song to help her son appreciate the bread that he leaves on his plate. Bilingual text.

Everybody Cooks Rice by Norah Dooley
A young girl discovers that all of her neighbors, despite their different backgrounds, eat rice. (See also *Everybody Brings Noodles* and *Everybody Bakes Bread* by the same author.)

Little Pea by Amy Krouse Rosenthal
Little Pea's parents insist that he finish eating all of his candy before he can have dessert—a big bowl of spinach!

Skill Focus
Phonological Awareness
(Beginning Sounds; Rhythm,
Rhyme, and Repetition)
Vocabulary

Theme Connections
Food
Opposites

"Peas Porridge Hot"

What to Do

- Tell the children that porridge is a cereal. People like to eat porridge cooked in different ways.
- Ask the children to listen carefully to the following poem to see how people like to eat their porridge. Recite the poem twice.

Peas Porridge Hot
Peas porridge hot,
Peas porridge cold,
Peas porridge in the pot
Nine days old.
Some like it hot.
Some like it cold.
Some like it in the pot
Nine days old!

- Ask, *How do some people like their porridge? How do other people like their porridge? How would you like to eat porridge?*
- Ask the children to clap the syllables in the words as you say the poem together.

Vocabulary

cold	old
cook	poem
eat	porridge
hot	pot
listen	rhyme
nine	

Materials

none needed

Click on the
*Between the
Lions* website!
pbskids.org/lions/gryphonhouse

Video Clip: Opposite Bunny:
hot/cold, chilly/warm
Game: Hopposites

"Gingerbread Cookies... Yummy!"

Skill Focus
Phonological Awareness (Rhythm and Repetition)
Sequencing
Vocabulary

Theme Connections
Food
Sounds

Vocabulary

bake
cookie cutter
cookies
cut
delicious
dough
eat
gingerbread
oven
roll
tasty
tummy
yummy

Materials

chart paper
markers or crayons

Click on the *Between the Lions* website!
pbskids.org/lions/gryphonhouse

Story: Edna Bakes Cookies
Video Clip: Opposite Bunny: yucky/yummy

What to Do

- Ask the children, *How do gingerbread cookies taste in your tummy?* Say, *Yes! Gingerbread cookies are yummy. They are delicious. They are tasty. That means they taste great!*

- Teach the children "Gingerbread Cookies...Yummy!" The children can invent motions to do with each line (roll the dough, cut the cookies, and so on).

> **Gingerbread Cookies...Yummy!**
> *(A variation of "Peanut Butter and Jelly")*
> First you take the dough and you roll it; you roll it.
> Gingerbread cookies...yummy!
>
> You take a cookie cutter and you cut it; you cut it.
> Gingerbread cookies...yummy!
>
> You put the cookies in the oven and you bake 'em;
>   you bake 'em.
> Gingerbread cookies...yummy!
>
> Then you pick up a cookie and you eat it; you eat it.
> Gingerbread cookies...yummy!

- Write the song on chart paper. Ask the children to point to the words that are repeated in the song.

Skill Focus
Name Recognition
Phonological Awareness (Rhythm and Repetition)

Theme Connection
Friends

"These Are Our Friends"

What to Do
☑ Have the children sit in a circle.
☑ Practice singing the chorus of "These Are Our Friends" with the class.

These Are Our Friends
(Tune: "The Addams Family" Theme Song)
Chorus:
These are our friends. (*clap, clap*)
This is our class. (*clap, clap*)
These are our friends. These are our friends.
This is our class. (*clap, clap*)

There's (child's name) and there's (child's name).
There's (child's name) and there's (child's name).
There's (child's name) and there's (child's name).
We're glad you're in our class.

☑ Sing the second verse as you go around the circle, pointing to the first six children and saying their names.
☑ Sing the chorus together after each verse.
☑ In the final verse, continue to go around the circle, repeating some of the names from the beginning of the song if necessary to fill the six slots.

Extension Idea
Instead of clapping your hands during the chorus, slap your arms or legs, or tap the floor. You may want to do a different action each time you repeat the chorus.

Vocabulary

chorus   friend
clap   glad
class   happy

Materials

none needed

Click on the
Between the Lions website!
pbskids.org/lions/gryphonhouse

Stories:
☒ Owen and Mzee
☒ Yo! Yes?

"Five Little Friends"

Skill Focus
Counting
Fine Motor Skills
Phonological Awareness (Rhyme, Rhythm, and Repetition)
Vocabulary

Theme Connection
Friends

Vocabulary

climbing	none
five	one
floor	run
four	sun
friends	swimming
jumped	three
little	tired
nap	two

Materials

none needed

What to Do

▣ Before reciting the fingerplay, ask the children to hold up a hand.

▣ Ask, *How many fingers are on your hand?* Wiggle each finger as you count: *1, 2, 3, 4, 5!*

▣ Say, *Let's recite a poem about five little friends.*

▣ Teach the children the fingerplay, "Five Little Friends."

Five Little Friends
Five little friends playing on the floor, (*Hold up five fingers.*)
One got tired, and then there were four. (*Hold up four fingers.*)
Four little friends climbing in a tree,
One jumped down, and then there were three. (*Hold up three fingers.*)
Three little friends skipping to the zoo,
One went for lunch, and then there were two. (*Hold up two fingers.*)
Two little friends swimming in the sun,
One went home, and then there was one. (*Hold up one finger.*)
One little friend going for a run,
One took a nap, and then there were none. (*Make a zero with thumb and index finger.*)

▣ Repeat the fingerplay with the children. Pause before saying the rhyming word at the end of every other line so the children can say the rhyming word.

Skill Focus

Gross Motor Skills
Phonological Awareness (Rhythm
and Repetition)
Social and Emotional Awareness

Theme Connection

Friends

"Let's Find a Friend"

What to Do

▣ Have the children stand in a circle.
▣ Sing the first verse of "Let's Find a Friend."

Let's Find a Friend
(*Tune: "Farmer in the Dell"*)
Let's find a friend.
Let's find a friend.
Hi-ho! the derry-o!
Let's find a friend.

(Mackenzie) find a friend.
(Mackenzie) find a friend.
Hi-ho! the derry-o!
(Mackenzie) find a friend.

We all found a friend,
We all found a friend,
Hi-ho! the derry-o!
We all found a friend.

▣ Choose a child in the circle and hold his hand. Together, walk
around the circle and sing the second verse of the song,
inserting the child's name in the first, second, and last lines.
▣ Invite the child to choose another friend, hold her hand, and
walk around the circle as you sing another verse with the new
friend's name.
▣ Repeat until everyone is holding hands and walking around
the room. Then sing the final verse together.

Vocabulary

circle	greet
find	handshake
found	name
friend	walk

Materials

none needed

Click on the
*Between the
Lions* website!
pbskids.org/lions/gryphonhouse

Stories:
▣ Owen and Mzee
▣ Yo! Yes?

"Hand in Hand"

Skill Focus
Gross Motor Skills
Phonological Awareness (Rhythm and Repetition)
Vocabulary

Theme Connection
Helping

Vocabulary

better	hand
big	jump
buddy	little
clap	march
different	read
friend	together
good	

Materials

none needed

What to Do

- Ask the children to stand and hold their buddy's hand (see page 17).
- Prompt the children to do the motions as you chant "Hand in Hand."

Hand in Hand
By myself I'm good, but together we're much better,
Together we're much better, hand in hand. (*Buddies hold hands.*)
By myself I can jump, but together we're better, (*Buddies let go of hands and then jump.*)
Together we're much better, hand in hand. (*Buddies hold hands.*)
Oh, big hands, little hands, clapping hands, and waving hands, (*Children let go of hands and clap, wave.*)
All different kinds of hands, together hand in hand. (*Buddies hold hands.*)

By myself I can march, but together we're much better, (*Buddies let go of hands and march in place.*)
Together we're much better, hand in hand. (*Buddies hold hands.*)
By myself I can read, but together we're much better, (*Buddies let go of hands and pretend to hold a book.*)
Together we're much better, hand in hand. (*Buddies hold hands.*)

- Recite the poem again, emphasizing the sound /h/. Invite the children to chant along with you.
- Display and review the Friends-Together class chart (see page 19). Encourage the children to make up new verses to "Hand in Hand" by substituting activities from the chart. For example, By myself I can *play house*, but together we're much better…

Skill Focus
Phonological Awareness
(Alliteration, Beginning
Sounds)

Theme Connections
Music
Sounds

"My Mom Makes Music"

What to Do

◻ Chant the first two lines of "My Mom Makes Music."

My Mom Makes Music
(*Tune: "The Mexican Hat Dance"*)
On Monday, my mom makes music.
My mom makes music with me.
On Monday, my mom makes music.
My mom makes music with me.
La-la-la-la-la-la-la la-la
Ma-ma-ma-ma-ma-ma-ma Ma-ma
La-la la-la-la la-la la-la
Ma-ma ma-ma-ma ma-ma Ma-ma!

◻ Repeat the lines very slowly, asking children to clap their hands each time they hear a word that begins with the /m/ sound, such as *music*. Teach the song as an alliterative chant, and then sing it. Invite the children to play an instrument during the chorus: *La la la la la…*

Vocabulary

begin	Monday
chant	music
chorus	sound
clap	word
mom	

Materials

none needed

Click on the
*Between the
Lions* website!
pbskids.org/lions/gryphonhouse

Game: Theo's Puzzles (m)

"Our Preschool Has a Band"

Skill Focus
Following Directions
Phonological Awareness (Rhythm and Repetition)
Vocabulary

Theme Connections
Music/Musical Instruments
Sounds

Vocabulary

band	play
beat	pluck
conductor	practice
drum	preschool
everywhere	signal
guitar	stop
instrument	

Materials

drum
rubber-band guitar

Click on the *Between the Lions* website!

pbskids.org/lions/gryphonhouse

Story: What Instrument Does Alvin Play
Poem: Tuning Up
Video Clip: Fred: Musical Instruments
Game: Dub Cubs

What to Do

◻ Introduce "Our Preschool Has a Band."

Our Preschool Has a Band
(*Tune: "Old MacDonald Has a Farm"*)
Our preschool has a band, ee-i-ee-i-o!
And in our band there is a drum, ee-i-ee-i-o!
With a *<beat, beat>* here, (*Children play drum.*)
And a *<beat, beat>* there, (*Children play drum.*)
Here a *<beat>*, there a *<beat>*,
Everywhere a *<beat, beat>*.
Our preschool has a band, ee-i-ee-i-o!

Our preschool has a band, ee-i-ee-i-o!
And in our band there is a guitar, ee-i-ee-i-o!
With a *<pluck, pluck>* here, (*Children play rubber-band guitar.*)
And a *<pluck, pluck>* there,
Here a *<pluck>*, there a *<pluck>*,
Everywhere a *<pluck, pluck>*.
Our preschool has a band, ee-i-ee-i-o!

With a *<beat, beat>* here, (*Children play drum.*)
And a *<beat, beat>* there,
Here a *<beat>*, there a *<beat>*,
Everywhere a *<beat, beat>*.
Our preschool has a band, ee-i-ee-i-o!

◻ You are the conductor. First establish hand signals for "play" and "stop" and let children practice following the signals. Then sing the song together.

◻ As you sing the name of each instrument, point to the children with that instrument and have them play the sound. After singing and playing, congratulate the musicians!

Skill Focus
Making Connections
Phonological Awareness
(Rhythm, Rhyme, and
Repetition)

Theme Connection
Music

Sing-a-Song Sack

Preparation
▣ Select objects that will remind the children of songs that they
know (see the list in the chart that follows).
▣ Place the objects in a bag.

What to Do
▣ Tell the children that singing is one of your favorite ways to
make music.
▣ Ask the children to recall some of the songs they have sung
together.
▣ Introduce the Sing-a-Song Sack. Say, *Inside this sack are things
that will remind you of songs we have sung.*
▣ Invite a child to reach in the bag and pull out an object.
▣ Encourage the children to raise their hand if they can think of
a song about the object. Together sing the song(s). Some
possibilities are:

Vocabulary

favorite   remind
object   sing
remember

Materials

bag
objects that are related to songs
that the children know

Objects	Songs
star	"Twinkle, Twinkle, Little Star"
dog	"Bingo" "Oh, Where, Oh, Where Has My Little Dog Gone?" "How Much Is That Doggie in the Window?" "Rags"
book	"Read, Read, Read a Book" (see page 67)
sock	"The Laundry Basket"

Objects	Songs
letter	The ABC Song" "Oh Where, Oh Where Has the Alphabet Gone?" (see page 197)
train	"Down by the Station" "I've Been Working on the Railroad"
cow	"The Farmer in the Dell" "Old MacDonald Had a Farm"
duck	"Five Little Ducks"
pail	"Jack and Jill"
lamb	"Mary Had a Little Lamb"
monkey	"Ten Little Monkeys Jumping on the Bed"
bus	"The Wheels on the Bus"

Extension Idea

Take an object from the bag and challenge the children to make up a song about the object.

Skill Focus
Phonological Awareness
(Rhyming)
Vocabulary

Theme Connections
My Neighborhood
Food
Sounds

"Going Shopping"

What to Do

▣ Tell the children that the poem you are going to recite, "Going Shopping," is fun to say because some of the words rhyme. Remind them that words rhyme when they have the same sound at the end.

▣ Recite "Going Shopping."

Going Shopping

Come go to the store
   with me,
It's just down the street.
We don't need a car,
We can go on our feet.
Daddy wants apples
And onions and steak,
Mother wants bread
And strawberry cake.

Brother wants chicken
And fish and potatoes.
I want cereal
And lettuce and tomatoes.
Come go to the store with
   me,
It's just down the street.
We don't need a car,
We can go on our feet.

▣ Read the poem again and ask the children to listen for the rhyming words. You may want to emphasize the rhyming words by whispering them.

▣ Say, *Listen to these two words*—street *and* feet. *Say the two words after me*—street, feet. *The words* street *and* feet *rhyme because they sound the same at the end*—/eet/.

▣ Ask the children to complete the sentence: *I walk down the street on my* _____.

▣ Recite the poem again. Pause before the second word in a rhyming pair and invite the children to chime in (*street/feet*; *steak/cake*; *potatoes/tomatoes*).

Vocabulary

apples	potatoes
bread	recite
brother	rhyme
car	shop
cereal	shopping
chicken	sound
daddy	steak
feet	store
fish	strawberry
lettuce	cake
mother	street
onions	tomatoes
poem	

Materials

none needed

Click on the
*Between the
Lions* website!
pbskids.org/lions/gryphonhouse

Song: Bee-bim Bop!
Game: Monkey Match (rhymes)

3+

"All the Pretty Little Horses"

Skill Focus
Phonological Awareness (Rhythm and Rhyme)

Theme Connection
Nighttime

Vocabulary

asleep	little
bay	lullaby
black	pretty
cry	sleep
dapple	song
gray	wake
horse	

Materials

none needed

What to Do

▣ Tell the children you are going to sing them another lullaby.

▣ Remind them that lullabies are songs that help people fall asleep.

▣ Sing "All the Pretty Little Horses" or another favorite lullaby.

> **All the Pretty Little Horses**
> (*Tune: Traditional*)
> Hush-a-bye, don't you cry,
> Go to sleep, my little baby.
> When you wake
> You shall have
> All the pretty little horses.
>
> Blacks and bays, dapples and grays,
> All the pretty little horses.
> Hush-a-bye, don't you cry,
> Go to sleep, my little baby.

▣ As you sing the song again, ask the children to clap their hands (or make a snoring sound!) each time they hear the word *sleep*.

Skill Focus

Active Listening

Phonological Awareness (Rhythm and Rhyme)

Vocabulary

Theme Connections

Nighttime

Animals

"Night Bird"

What to Do

▣ Tell the children you are going to read them a poem that is also a riddle.

▣ Ask them to listen carefully to the clues to figure out the answer to the riddle.

▣ Tell the children to wait until you finish reading the poem before saying their answer. Recite "Night Bird" without reading the title.

> **Night Bird**
> I fly through the night sky,
> With swooping wings,
> And glowing eyes.
> I circle low, I circle high.
> Listen to my midnight cry.
> Who, who, who, am I?

▣ Invite the children to guess who the poem is about.

▣ Ask the children to act like swooping owls, circling high and low, as you read the poem a second time.

▣ Explain that the word *midnight* means "very late in the night when most people are sleeping."

Vocabulary

answer	owl
circle	poem
clue	riddle
cry	sky
eye	slowing
fly	swooping
midnight	wing
night	

Materials

none needed

"The Grand Old Duke of York"

Skill Focus
Gross Motor Skills
Phonological Awareness (Rhythm and Repetition)
Vocabulary (Opposites, Positional Words)

Theme Connection
Opposites

Vocabulary

above	neither
down	nor
halfway	opposite
hill	ten thousand
march	up
men	

Materials

none needed

What to Do

- Have the children stand up.
- Point your finger above your head and ask, *What is the opposite of* up? Point at the ground as you say, *Yes, the opposite of* up *is* down.
- Tell the children you are going to sing a song about marching up and down a hill.
- Sing or chant the first verse of "The Grand Old Duke of York" with enthusiasm.

> **The Grand Old Duke of York**
> The Grand Old Duke of York
> He had ten thousand men. (*Hold up ten fingers.*)
> He marched them up to the top of the hill, (*Point up.*)
> And he marched them down again. (*Point down.*)
> And when they were up, they were up. (*Stand tall.*)
> And when they were down, they were down. (*Crouch way down.*)
> And when they were only halfway up, (*Rise halfway up.*)
> They were neither up nor down. (*Open arms and shrug.*)

- Invite the children to join in as you sing the song again. Add the movements.
- Sing the song again. This time, pause each time the words *up* and *down* are used in the song and ask the children to fill in the word.

Click on the
*Between the
Lions* website!
pbskids.org/lions/gryphonhouse

Game: Hopposites

Skill Focus
Following Directions
Phonological Awareness
Vocabulary (Opposites)

Theme Connection
Opposites

"Big and Small"

What to Do

▣ Have the children sit on their knees and roll into a little ball. Tell them to move their bodies to become as big as possible, the opposite of small.

▣ Ask the children to become as little as a teeny-weeny mouse!

▣ Invite the children to act out the poem "Big and Small" as you read it.

> **Big and Small**
> I can make myself real big, (*Stand up on toes.*)
> By standing up straight and tall.
> But when I am tired of being big,
> I can make myself get small. (*Stoop down.*)

▣ Say the poem again. Ask the children to listen for the words that are the same (big/big) and the words that rhyme (tall/small).

Extension Idea

Have the children stand in a line at a distance facing you. Review or teach words that mean "big" (*gigantic, enormous, giant, huge*) and "little" (*small, tiny, itsy-bitsy, baby*). Prompt the children to ask you if they can take steps forward and what kind of steps they would like to take. For example, *Teacher, may I take three little steps?* Encourage the children to use different words for *big* and *little. May I take five* itsy-bitsy *steps? May I take one* enormous *step?* The game ends when the children reach you.

Vocabulary

baby	myself
ball	opposite
big	roll up
enormous	sit
giant	small
gigantic	standing up
help	steps
huge	tall
itsy-bitsy	teeny-weeny
knees	tiny
little	tired

Materials

none needed

Click on the *Between the Lions* website!
pbskids.org/lions/gryphonhouse

Video Clips:
▣ My Favorite Word (humongous)
▣ My Favorite Word (miniscule)
Game: Hopposites

"Opposite Song"

Skill Focus
Phonological Awareness
(Rhythm, Rhyme, and
Repetition)
Vocabulary (Opposites)

Theme Connection
Opposites

Vocabulary

bye	no
dry	nod
fun	opposites
game	slow
go	stop
hi	wet
high	yes
low	

Materials

none needed

Click on the
*Between the
Lions* website!
pbskids.org/lions/gryphonhouse

Video Clip: Opposite Bunny:
    fast/slow
Game: Hopposites

What to Do

▣ Before singing the song, tell the children you are going to play an opposite game.

▣ Say, *Watch what I do. Instead of doing what I do, I want you to do the opposite.* Nod your head yes as you say, *I'm nodding my head yes. Now you do the opposite.*

▣ Ask, *What are you doing? You are shaking your head no.*

▣ Sit down as you say, *I'm sitting down. Now you do the opposite.* Ask, *What are you doing? You are standing up.*

▣ Sing the "Opposite Song." As you sing the second and third verses, pause before the opposite words and prompt the children to say them.

> **The Opposite Song**
> (*Tune: "Do You Know The Muffin Man?"*)
> Oh, do you know some opposites,
> Some opposites,
> Some opposites?
> Oh, do you know some opposites?
> Opposites are fun.
>
> If I say *stop*,
> Then you say *go*.
> If I say *yes*,
> Then you say *no*.
> If I say *fast*,
> Then you say *slow*.
> Oh, opposites are fun.

▣ After singing, say the first word in each opposite pair and prompt the children to say the opposite word. For example, say *stop*. Children say *go*. Repeat with *yes/no*, *fast/slow*, *low/high*, *hi/bye*, and *wet/dry*.

Skill Focus

Making Connections
Phonological Awareness (Rhythm
and Rhyme)
Vocabulary

Theme Connections

Sounds
Nighttime

"Night Sneaks In"

AGE
3+

What to Do

- Ask the children, *When it's time to go to bed at night, do you ever want to stay up and keep playing?*
- Tell the children you are going to read a poem about a girl who lives in the country and doesn't want to go to sleep. The poem is about all the sounds the girl hears at night.
- Say, *We often think of the night as a quiet time. But if we listen very carefully, we can hear lots of sounds.*
- Recite "Night Sneaks In." Explain that a *symphony* is music made by lots of different instruments being played together.

    Night Sneaks In
    Night sneaks in when the sun goes down.
    The sky turns dark in my country town.
    The owl swoops from tree to tree.
    A symphony of sounds calls to me.
    The frog sings *reek reek* and jumps about.
    The pig snuffles with his snout.
    I'd like to stay up and play and play,
    But it's time to sleep until the next day.

- Ask, *What sounds do you hear at night?*

Extension Idea

As you read the poem again, ask the children to listen for the words that rhyme (down/town, tree/me, about/snout, and play/day). Challenge the children to name other words that rhyme with one of these rhyming word pairs.

Vocabulary

country	sky
day	sleep
down	sneak
frog	snuffle
night	sound
pig	sun
play	symphony
reek	

Materials

none needed

Click on the
*Between the
Lions* website!
pbskids.org/lions/gryphonhouse

Stories:
- Night in the Country
- Tabby Cat at Night

"Eenie Meenie Mynie Mo"

Skill Focus
Phonological Awareness
(Alliteration, Beginning
Sounds)

Theme Connections
Sounds
Rhymes

Vocabulary

clap
hear
marshmallow
monkey

rhyme
same
sound
word

Materials

none needed

What to Do

☒ Teach the children the following rhyme:

> Eenie Meenie Mynie Mo
> A monkey ate my marshmallow.

☒ Say the rhyme very slowly, asking the children to clap when they
hear a word that begins with the /m/ sound.

☒ Chant the rhyme at a normal pace and clap to the rhythm.

☒ Make up a melody and sing the rhyme together.

Extension Ideas

☒ Suggest that the children draw a picture or dictate a story about
what the monkey might do after eating a marshmallow.

☒ Challenge the children to change this rhyme to focus on other
beginning word sounds. For example:

> Eenie Teenie Tynie Toe
> A tiger ate my tomato.

> Eenie Beenie Bynie Blum
> A bobcat ate my _____. (bubblegum)

> Eenie Leenie Lynie Lop
> A leopard ate my _____. (lollipop)

> Eenie Seenie Synie Stoop
> A seagull ate my salty _____. (soup)

Click on the
*Between the
Lions* website!
pbskids.org/lions/gryphonhouse

Game: Theo's Puzzles (m)

Skill Focus
Following Directions
Phonological Awareness (Rhythm and Repetition)
Vocabulary

Theme Connections
Sounds

"John Jacob Jingleheimer Schmidt"

What to Do

◼ Teach the name, John Jacob Jingleheimer Schmidt, by having the children repeat after you:

John Jacob
John Jacob Jingle (*Pretend to ring a bell.*) heimer
John Jacob Jingle (*Pretend to ring a bell.*) heimer Schmidt

◼ Sing the song and invite the children to join in.

John Jacob Jingleheimer Schmidt
John Jacob Jingleheimer Schmidt,
His name is my name too.
Whenever we go out,
The people always shout,
"There goes John Jacob Jingleheimer Schmidt!"

Chorus (*Sing loudly!*): Da da-da da-da da-da!

◼ Tell the children that this song is sung in a special way. You sing it four times.
1. Sing the whole song in a nice loud voice.
2. Sing it in an "indoor voice," until you come to the last line, which you sing very loudly: **Da da-da da-da da-da!**
3. Sing it in a whisper, until you come to the last line, which you sing very loudly: **Da da-da da-da da-da!**
4. Sing it silently, just moving your mouth, until you come to the last line, which you sing very loudly: **Da da-da da-da da-da!**

◼ Sing the song again, emphasizing the beginning sound of /j/ in the first three names. Challenge the children to think of other names and words that begin with the /j/ sound.

Vocabulary

bell	repeat
listen	ring
jingle	shout
loud	silently
name	whisper

Materials

none needed

Click on the *Between the Lions* website!
pbskids.org/lions/gryphonhouse

Game: Theo's Puzzles (j)

Finish the Rhyme

Skill Focus
Phonological Awareness (Rhythm and Rhyme)

Theme Connection
Sounds

Vocabulary

beat	quack
blow	stomp
clap	suck
drum	touch
pluck	

Materials

none needed

What to Do

◼ Chant the following verses. Pause to let the children provide the final rhyming word.

Drum, drum, drum.
Don't suck your _____. (*Hint: Hold up your thumb.*)

Beat, beat, beat.
Now stomp your _____. (*Hint: Point at your feet.*)

Pluck, pluck, pluck.
Now quack like a _____.

Blow, blow, blow.
Now touch your _____. (*Hint: Point at your toe.*)

Clap, clap, clap.
Put your hands in your _____. (*Hint: Point to your lap.*)

◼ Add another sound element to this activity by playing a drum for the first two verses, a rubber-band guitar for the third verse, and a cardboard tube horn for the fourth verse.

Skill Focus

Phonological Awareness (Alliteration, Beginning Sounds)

Theme Connection

Sounds

Alliteration

What to Do

- Ask the children to listen to the words as you say this sentence: *I buy big books.*
- Prompt the children to say the sentence with you, emphasizing the /b/ sound at the beginning of the words.
- Invite the children to say the sentence with you faster and faster. Say, *Some of the words begin with the same sound. The word* buy *begins with the /b/ sound. The word* big *starts with the /b/ sound, too. So does the word* books. *Brian and Bridget, your names begin with the /b/ sound, too!*

  Note: On other days, focus on another letter using a sentence such as *I feel fingerpaint on my fingernails* or *No nightingales are napping in the nest.*

Extension Idea

Hold a toy or handmade microphone in front of your mouth and say the sentence loudly and clearly. Have the children say the sentence with you, stretching the /b/ sounds. Then invite them to take turns saying words that start with /b/ into the microphone. For support, you may want to provide objects that begin with the /b/ sound.

Vocabulary

beginning	miss
emphasize	my
fast	sentence
faster	sound
mama	word

Material

toy or handmade microphone

Click on the *Between the Lions* website! pbskids.org/lions/gryphonhouse

Game: Theo's Puzzles

Lionel and Leona Letter Poster

Skill Focus
Phonological Awareness
(Beginning Sounds)

Theme Connection
Sounds

Vocabulary

begin	objects
catalog	pictures
chart	sound
magazine	

Materials

magazine and catalogs
scissors
poster board
glue or tape

Preparation

☑ Cut out pictures of objects that begin with the /l/ sound from magazines and catalogs.

☑ Make a chart with pictures of objects that begin with the /l/ sound (lion, lake, lemon). Place a picture of Leona and Lionel at the top of the poster.

Lionel and Leona's Letter Poster

Leona

Lionel

lemon

lion

ladybug

leaf

◪ Gather pictures of other objects that begin with the /l/ sound and a few that do not.

What to Do

◪ Point to the pictures of Leona and Lionel, the lion cubs in *Between the Lions.*

◪ Have the children repeat their names after you, emphasizing the initial /l/ sound. Say, Leona *begins with the /l/ sound.* Lionel *also begins with the /l/ sound. If your name begins with the same sound as Lionel and Leona, please stand up.* Add these children's names to the chart.

◪ Explain that you will be placing on the chart pictures of objects that begin with the /l/ sound. Show the first picture to the children and ask, *Does* lemon *begin with the same sound as* Lionel *and* Leona? Say each word slowly—*lemon, Lionel, Leona*—emphasizing the /l/ sound. Attach the picture to the chart.

◪ Repeat the process with the remaining pictures.

◪ Review the completed chart with the children, pointing to each object as you slowly say its name.

◪ Encourage the children to add to the poster throughout the day or for as long as it is posted in the classroom.
Note: On other days, work with the children to create charts that focus on other letters.

Click on the
*Between the
Lions* website!
pbskids.org/lions/gryphonhouse

Games:
◪ Monkey Match (beginning sounds)
◪ Theo's Puzzles (l)

Tongue Twisters

Skill Focus
Phonological Awareness (Alliteration, Beginning Sounds)

Theme Connection
Sounds

Vocabulary

beginning	same
fast	sentence
faster	sound
pop	tongue
popcorn	tongue twister
pot	word

Materials

none needed

Click on the *Between the Lions* website!
pbskids.org/lions/gryphonhouse

Video Clips:
- Choppers Chop, Shoppers Shop
- This is the sixth sister.

What to Do

- Encourage the children to have fun trying to say a tongue twister, such as *This is the sixth sister* or *Sammy sees the setting sun.*
- Repeat the words slowly, emphasizing the /s/ sound at the beginning of the words. Have the children say the sentence with you faster and faster.
- Point out the /s/ sound at the beginning of the words. Say, *I notice that some of the words begin with the same sound. The word* sixth *begins with the /s/ sound. The word* sister *starts with the /s/ sound, too. Samantha, your name begins with the /s/ sound, too!*
- Encourage the children to have fun trying to say one of the following tongue twisters:

  Rubber baby buggy bumpers
  Nat's knapsack strap snapped.
  Zack's backpack lacks Zack's snacks.
  Shelly sells seashells.
  She sees cheese; sheep see cheese.
  Gus's buzzard busted Buzz's buzzer.
  Scram, clam, scram
  Mom shops for Pop's socks.
  Mixed biscuits
  Choppers chop, droppers drop, shoppers shop.
  Ten men spent ten cents.
  Twenty men spent twenty cents.

Extension Idea

Challenge the children to repeat any of the tongue twisters three times fast, or to make up their own tongue twister.

Skill Focus
Phonological Awareness
(Beginning Sounds)

Theme Connection
Sounds

Bag of /r/ Sounds

What to Do

- Tell the children that the letter "Rr" makes the /r/ sound. Say, Running rabbits *is fun to say because it has lots of /r/ sounds.*
- Say the words again slowly, emphasizing the /r/ sound. Ask, *Can you hear the /r/ sound?* Say the word *rabbits* again, emphasizing the initial /r/ sound: *rrrrabbits!*
- Display a bag or bucket, along with small items that begin with the /r/ sound, such as a rope, ruler, and pictures of a rabbit or rake, and a few items that do not begin with the /r/ sound (crayon, fork, glue). Name each item.
- Tell the children that only things that begin with the /r/ sound belong in the bag or bucket. Hold up the rock and ask, *Does the word* rock *begin with the same sound as the word* rope? Say, *rock, rope. Yes, they both begin with the /r/ sound. Who would like to put the rock in the bucket?*
- Ask the children to pick up an object, name it, and say whether it belongs in the bag or bucket.
- Continue until all the items have been sorted.

Extension Idea

Challenge the children to find things in the classroom that begin with the /r/ sound. Repeat with other letter sounds.

Vocabulary

belongs	rhyme
crayon	rock
fork	rope
glue	rug
object	ruler
rabbit	same
rake	sound

Materials

bag or bucket

items (or pictures of items) that begin with the /r/ sound (rock, rope, ruler, rabbit, rake)

items that do not begin with the /r/ sound (crayon, fork, glue)

Click on the *Between the Lions* website!
pbskids.org/lions/gryphonhouse

Song: Rocket-Doodle-Doo
Video Clip: Fred Says: rooster
Game: Theo's Puzzles (r)

4+

More Alliteration

Skill Focus
Phonological Awareness
(Alliteration, Beginning
Sounds)

Theme Connection
Sounds

Vocabulary

cat	makes
car	mama
cookie	Monday
beginning	morning
emphasize	muffins
fast	my
faster	sound
identify	

Materials

none needed

What to Do

☑ Ask the children to listen to the words as you say this sentence:
My cat complains about cookies in the car.

☑ Prompt the children to say the sentence with you, emphasizing the /c/ sound at the beginning of the words.

☑ Invite the children to say the sentence with you faster and faster. Identify the /c/ sounds in each word.

Extension Ideas

☑ Say the sentence again slowly, pausing between each word. Give the children blank index cards on which you have written "C." Tell the children to hold up the letter card when they hear a word that begins with the /c/ sound.

☑ Serve cookies for a snack.

Click on the
*Between the
Lions* website!
pbskids.org/lions/gryphonhouse

Song: The Two Sounds Made
by c
Game: Theo's Puzzles (c)

Skill Focus
Letter Recognition
Phonological Awareness
(Alliteration, Beginning
Sounds)
Word Recognition

Theme Connection
Sounds

Yo! Yes! Yow!

What to Do

- As the children watch, write the words *Yo! Yes! Yow!* in big letters on chart paper.
- Point to each word as you read it aloud with enthusiasm.
- Have the children repeat the words with you.
- Ask the children to identify the first letter in the words *yo, yes,* and *yow.*
- Repeat the words. Ask, *Can you hear the /y/ sound at the beginning of each word?*
- Say, *There are three words. Who can find the word yes? It's the second word, the one in the middle.*
- Recite "Tell Me What You Hear."

Tell Me What You Hear
Listen, listen, loud and clear (*Cup your hand to one ear.*)
What's the first sound that you hear?
Yo! Yes! Yow! (*Emphasize the /y/ sound.*)
Tell me, tell me, what you hear! (*Children say the /y/ sound.*)

Extension Idea

Use this same approach with other sounds. Write three words beginning with the same sound on chart paper, talk about the words, and then recite the poem with these three words in it.

Vocabulary

begin	loud
beginning	sound
clear	word
first	yes
hear	yo
identify	yow
letter	

Materials

chart paper
markers

Click on the
*Between the
Lions* website!
pbskids.org/lions/gryphonhouse

Song: Yo! Yes?
Video Clip: Opposite Bunny: yucky/yummy
Game: Theo's Puzzles (y)

Last Sound You Hear

Vocabulary

ball	hat
cat	jacket
cloud	lamp
cup	last
end	listen
ending	soap
foot	sound
hand	

Materials

six picture cards of objects, some that end with the /p/ sound and others that do not (for example: cup, cloud, soap, hand, lamp, ball)

Click on the *Between the Lions* website! pbskids.org/lions/gryphonhouse

Songs:
- ▣ If You Can Read (op)
- ▣ Sloppy Pop

Video Clip: Fred Says: rock/truck

Games:
- ▣ Dub Cubs
- ▣ Fuzzy Lion Ears

What to Do

▣ Play a listening game to help the children hear and recognize the sound at the end of words. The examples used in this activity are the /p/ and /t/ sounds.

▣ The /p/ sound:
- ▣ Ask the children to say the word *hop* with you. Have them hold their hand in front of their mouth and repeat the word. Ask, *Did you feel the puff of air on your hand at the end of the word? Let's try it again. Notice what you do with your lips when you say the /p/ sound at the end of the word* hop.
- ▣ Say, *I'm going to show you some picture cards. Tell me what you see on the card. Then tell me if the word ends in the /p/ sound.*
- ▣ Show the children six picture cards (cup, cloud, soap, hand, lamp, ball). After you show each card, ask the children what is on it. Then have them repeat the word. Ask, *Does the word* cup *end in the /p/ sound?*

▣ The /t/ sound:
- ▣ Ask the children to say the word *jacket* with you. Ask, *Did you tap your teeth with your tongue when you said the /t/ sound at the end of the word? Let's try it again.*
- ▣ Show the children a hat. Ask, *What is this? Let's say the word together:* hat. *Did you hear the /t/ sound at the end of* hat?
- ▣ Repeat the process with the words *foot* and *cat*.

Extension Idea

Challenge the children to find objects in the classroom that end with the /p/ or /t/ sound. Then try this activity with other ending sounds, such as /d/, /g/, /l/, /m/, /n/, and /s/.

Skill Focus
Phonological Awareness
(Rhyming)

Theme Connection
Sounds

Pop and Stop

Preparation
▣ Write the words of "Popcorn Chant" on chart paper.

What to Do
▣ Recite "Popcorn Chant" to the children, pointing to each word as you say it.

Popcorn Chant
Popcorn popper,
Pop, pop, pop!
Popcorn popper,
Do not stop!
Poppity, boppity, pop, pop, pop.
Hoppity, poppity, hop, hop, hop.
Dop and a loppity,
Lop and a doppity,
Pop and a boppity,
Stop, pop, stop.

▣ Point to the word *pop* in the second line of the chant and the word *stop* in the fourth line.
▣ Highlight the rhyming words with a yellow highlighter. Ask the children to repeat the words with you.
▣ Tell the children that the words *pop* and *stop* rhyme because they sound the same at the end. They both end with /op/.
▣ Say, *I'm going to say some words. Listen carefully. If the word I say rhymes with the word* pop, *I want you to pop up. If it doesn't rhyme, sit still. Say the word* stop. Ask, *Does* stop *rhyme with* pop? Pop, stop. *They rhyme! Let's all pop up!* Repeat the process with the words *bop, mop, top,* and *pigeon.*

Vocabulary

chant	popper
dop	rhyme
end	rhyming
highlight	same
hop	sound
lop	stop
pop	word
popcorn	

Materials

chart paper
markers
yellow highlighter

Click on the
*Between the
Lions* website!
pbskids.org/lions/gryphonhouse

Songs:
▣ If You Can Read (op)
▣ Sloppy Pop

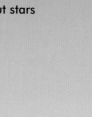

Plurals

Vocabulary

end	sound
one	star
more than	two
plural	

Materials

cut-out stars

What to Do

☑ Talk about the concept of plurals as you engage the children in a discussion about the sound they hear at the end of the word *stars*.

☑ Hold up a single cut-out star. Ask, *How many stars do I have in my hand? Yes, I have one star.* Have the children repeat the word *star* with you.

☑ Hold up two cut-out stars. Ask, *How many stars do I have now? I have two stars.*

☑ Ask the children to say the word *stars* with you, stretching the final /s/ sound: *starsssss*. Ask, *What sound do you hear at the end of the word* stars?

☑ Explain that sometimes when we hear the /s/ sound at the end of a word, it means that there is more than one. Say, *One star* (hold up a star); *two stars* (hold up two stars).

Extension Idea

Throughout the day, ask the children to find two similar objects in the classroom—two blocks, two crayons, two napkins, two trucks, and so on.

Click on the *Between the Lions* website!
pbskids.org/lions/gryphonhouse

Song: Without an S

Skill Focus
Active Listening
Phonological Awareness
(Rhyming)

Theme Connections
Sounds
Rhymes

Star Rhymes

What to Do

- Have the children sit in a circle. Give each child a cut-out star.
- Say, *I'm going to say some words. If a word rhymes with the word* star, *raise your star above your head.*
- Slowly say each of the following words: *car, sun, jar, far, Earth.* After each word, ask, *Does this word rhyme with the word* star? *If it does, raise your star!*
- Ask, *What other words can you think of that rhyme with the word* star?

Vocabulary

car	rhyme
Earth	star
far	sun
jar	word
raise	

Materials

cut-out stars, one for each child

Extension Idea

Show the children a basket filled with objects, including a star and a toy car. Ask a child to find the star. Then ask if he can find an object that rhymes with *star*. Display the two objects and say them aloud with the children: *star, car*.

Cleo and Theo's Book Suggestions

Coyote Places the Stars by Harriet Peck Taylor
A retelling of a Wasco Indian story about how coyote arranges the
    stars in the shapes of his animal friends.
How the Stars Fell into the Sky:
    A Navajo Legend by Jerrie Oughton
    This retelling of a Navajo folktale explains the patterns of the stars
    in the sky.
I Am a Star by Jean Marzollo
    Simple, poetic text and bright cut-paper illustrations explain facts
    about stars, including why we can't see stars during the day.
Our Stars by Anne Rockwell
    A young boy tells us about stars, constellations, planets, and outer
    space.

Click on the
*Between the
Lions* website!
pbskids.org/lions/gryphonhouse

Song: The a-r Song
Game: Monkey Match (rhymes)

AGE 4+ Onset and Rime Blends

Vocabulary

bird	first
blend	follow
book	sound
cat	syllable
dog	

Material

picture of a cat

Click on the
*Between the
Lions* website!
pbskids.org/lions/gryphonhouse

Song: If You Can Read
(at, en, op)
Poem: Brush Dance
Video Clips:

- Blending Bowl: dine
- Fred Says: hot

Games:

- Blending Bowl
- Dub Cubs

What to Do

- Listening to onset (all the sounds in a syllable that come before the first vowel) and rime (the first vowel in a syllable and all the sounds that follow) helps children to blend and segment words. Start by stretching out the onset and rime sounds in words.
- Say, *I'm going to say the name of an animal in a special way. Let's stretch out the word* cat.
- Say /c/ as you hold out one hand.
- Say /at/ as you hold out the other hand.
- Say *cat* as you place your hands together to show the blending of the two sounds. Show the children a picture of a cat.

Extension Idea

Play a listening game with the children to help them hear sounds in sequence and then blend them together to make a word. Tell the children that you are holding a picture of a mystery friend. Ask them to listen carefully and try to guess what or who the mystery friend is. Say, /d/ *(pause)* /og/. Tell the children to listen carefully and say the onset, /d/, and rime, /og/, again. Ask, *Can you guess our mystery friend?* Show the children a picture of a dog to confirm that they have guessed correctly. Repeat the process with the words *bird* (/b/ /ird/) and *book* (/b/ /ook/).

Skill Focus
Phonological Awareness (Onset and Rime)

Theme Connection
Sounds

Going on a Word Hunt

What to Do

▣ Play a listening game to help the children hear sounds in sequence and blend them to make a word.

▣ Tell the children to echo each line and copy the motions.

Teacher: Going on a word hunt. (*Teacher slaps thighs on each beat.*)

Children: Going on a word hunt. (*Children slap thighs on each beat.*)

Teacher: What's this word? (*Teacher slaps thighs on each beat.*)

Children: What's this word? (*Children slap thighs on each beat.*)

Teacher: /st/ (pause) /ars/ (*Make fist with right hand on /st/ and left hand on /ars/.*)

Children: /st/ (pause) /ars/ (*Make fist with left hand on /st/ and right hand on /ars/.*)

Together: *Stars!* (*Bring both fists together.*)

Cleo and Theo's Book Suggestions

The following books focus on listening to sounds:

City Lullaby by Marilyn Singer and Carll Cneut
Lively poems transform the sounds of the city into a lullaby for a sleepy baby.

The Listening Walk by Paul Showers and Aliki
A girl and her father take a special walk and listen to the sounds around them.

Sounds All Around by Wendy Pfeffer and Holly Keller
This book in the Let's-Read-and-Find-Out Science series offers a simple explanation of sounds and hearing, including how animals hear.

Sounds of the Wild: Nighttime by Maurice Pledger
This nonfiction book describes sounds made by night animals in different parts of the world.

Vocabulary

blend

copy

echo

hear

hunt

listen

sequence

sounds

word

Materials

none needed

Click on the *Between the Lions* website!

pbskids.org/lions/gryphonhouse

Games:

▣ Blending Bowl

▣ Fuzzy Lion Ears

▣ Monkey Match (beginning letter sounds, rhymes)

"Star Name Chant"

Skill Focus
Phonological Awareness
(Clapping Syllables in Names;
Rhythm, Rhyme, and
Repetition)
Shape Recognition

Theme Connection
Stars

Vocabulary

chant   part
clap   smile
little   syllable
name

Materials

scissors
yellow poster board

Preparation

☒ Cut out a large yellow star from yellow poster board.

What to Do

☒ Have the children sit in a circle.
☒ Hold up a large yellow star and ask the children what it is.
☒ Pass the star to the child sitting on your right and ask the child to hold it above her head.
☒ Recite the "Star Name Chant." On the third line, chant the name of the child holding the star.

> **Star Name Chant**
> Little star, little star,
> Who do you see?
> I see (Simone),
> Smiling at me.

☒ At the end chant, "S-I-M-O-N-E, Simone!"
☒ Have the child pass the star to the next child.
☒ Together, recite the chant with the new child's name. Repeat until each child has had a chance to hold the star.
☒ Try one of the following variations on the same day or another day:
  ☒ Have the children clap the beats or syllables in each child's name (*Si-mone*).
  ☒ Spell the letters in each child's name: *S-i-m-o-n-e*.

Skill Focus

Phonological Awareness (Blending and Segmenting Syllables)
Word Awareness (Compound Words)

Theme Connection

Stars

Word Magic

What to Do

- Give the children their star wands and tell them to get ready for some word magic!
- Play a sound game to help the children blend and segment the parts of compound words.
- Say, *Listen carefully to the words I am going to say. I'm going to say the parts of the word very slowly. See if you can put the parts together to guess the word.*
- Say *street/light* slowly, pausing for a few seconds between the two word parts. When the children guess the word, have them wave their magic wand. Show them a picture of a streetlight.
- Repeat the process with the words *headlight* and *skyscraper*.
- Invite the children to do some word magic by making the parts of compound words disappear.
- Ask the children to say the word *streetlight* with you. Then say, *Let's wave our star wands and say the word* streetlight *without* street. (light) *We just made the word* street *disappear!*
- Repeat with the words *headlight* and *skyscraper*.

Extension Idea

Write the words *light*, *head*, and *street* on word cards. Present each compound word by displaying a word card for each part. Say the whole word (*streetlight*), then wave your star wand and put the word card (*street*) behind your back. What word is left? (*light*)

Vocabulary

blend	skyscraper
compound	sound
headlight	star
magic	wand
segment	

Materials

pictures of a streetlight, a headlight, and a skyscraper
star wands, one for each child

Click on the *Between the Lions* website!
pbskids.org/lions/gryphonhouse

Video Clip: Arty Smartypants: snail/nail

Chapter 6

Understanding the Concepts of Print

This chapter of *Wild About Literacy* focuses on helping children learn that print conveys meaning and that there are many great reasons to read and to write (see The Literacy Scope and Sequence on pages 14–15). As they watch you read books, children notice that we read from top to bottom and from left to right. Song and poem charts, environmental print, and writing activities also help children learn about letters and words, the spaces between words, and the direction in which we read words on a page.

The activities in this chapter are grouped alphabetically by topic and then by age (3+ or 4+) within each topic or theme. The activities have the following components:

Skill Focus	**Materials**
Theme Connection(s)	**Preparation (if necessary)**
Vocabulary	**What to Do**

Skill Focus—lists the literacy skills that the activity addresses and other skills that young children need to learn, such as fine motor skills or emotional awareness.

Theme Connections—lists one or two familiar early childhood themes that the activity covers. If more than one theme is listed, the first is the one with the strongest connection.

Vocabulary—lists words that are part of the activity. Use these when you are engaging children in the activity, defining their meaning if necessary. Repeat these words throughout the day so children hear the words used in context and can begin to understand how each word is used.

Materials—lists, in alphabetical order, the materials you will need to do the activity. Be sure you have the materials you need before you begin the activity.

> **A Note About Repetition:** You will find the same songs, poems, and books used in multiple activities in *Wild About Literacy*. Children benefit and learn from repetition. When children hear a familiar song or poem, they may learn something new or solidify what they already know. Using a familiar song or story to teach a new skill is a technique used by many teachers, which is why you will find repetition in this book.

Preparation—If the activity needs any preparation, such as writing a song or poem on chart paper or preparing a chart, what you need to do is described in this section.

What to Do—Step by step, this section outlines how to engage children in the activity.

In addition, many activities include ideas that build on the main activity, extend it to another curriculum area, or suggest books that relate to the activity.

The following children's book is used in two activities in this chapter:
The Lion and the Mouse by Bernadette Watts (see pages 154 and 163)

In addition, many children's books are suggested as a way to extend an activity. Some of the book suggestions in this chapter include:
Bread Is for Eating
　　by David and Phillis Gershator and Emma Shaw-Smith
Bread, Bread, Bread by Ann Morris and Ken Heyman
Children's Quick and Easy Cookbook by Angela Wilkes
Cook and Learn: Recipes, Songs, and Activities for Children
　　by Adrienne Wiland
Dim Sum for Everyone! by Grace Lin
Dumpling Soup by Jama Kim Rattigan
Everybody Cooks Rice by Norah Dooley and Peter J. Thompson
I'm the Chef: A Young Chef 's Mexican Cookbook by Karen
　　Ward
Jalapeño Bagels by Natasha Wing and Robert Casilla
Let's Eat by Ana Zamorano, Amy Griffin, and Julie Vivas
Mama Provi and the Pot of Rice
　　by Sylvia Rosa-Casanova and Robert Roth
Pete's a Pizza
　　by William Steig [featured on a *Between the Lions* episode]
Pretend Soup and Other Real Recipes
　　by Mollie Katzen and Ann L. Henderson
Tortillas and Lullabies/Tortillas y cancioncitas
　　by Lynn Reiser and Corazones Valientes
Where Does Food Come From? by Shelley Rotner and Gary Goss

Click on the
*Between the
Lions* website!
pbskids.org/lions/gryphonhouse

Books About Reading
Books Featured on *Between
　　the Lions*
Recommended Books

Skill Focus

Concepts of Print (Directionality, Return Sweep)
Vocabulary
Word Recognition

Theme Connections

All About Me
Clothing

"I Can Do It Myself"

Preparation

☐ Write the poem "I Can Do It Myself" on chart paper.

What to Do

☐ Recite "I Can Do It Myself." As you recite each verse, have the children act out how to put on each item of clothing. Then display the poem chart.

I Can Do It Myself
Hat on head, just like this,
Pull it down, you see.
I can put my hat on all by
    myself,
Without any help, just me.

One arm in, two arms in,
Buttons one, two, and
    three.
I can put my jacket on all
    by myself,
Without any help, just me.

Toes in first, heels down
    next,
Pull and pull, then see—
I can put my boots on all
    by myself,
Without any help, just me.

Fingers there, thumbs
    right here,
Hands warm as can be.
I can put my mittens on all
    by myself,
Without any help, just me.

Vocabulary

arm	myself
boots	next
fingers	one
hands	three
hat	thumb
head	toes
heels	two
help	warm
jacket	without
mittens	

Materials

chart paper
markers

☐ Read aloud the title as you point to the words. Tell the children that these are the words to the poem you just recited.

☐ Tell the children you are going to recite the poem again. This time, instead of acting out the poem, you want them to look at the words. Ask, *Who can show me where I should start reading?*

☐ Recite the poem as you point to each word. Exaggerate the return sweep of your hand as you finish reading one line and begin another.

☐ Invite the children to act out the poem again as you read it once more.

"I Love to..." Class Chart

Skill Focus
Concepts of Print
Dictating Sentences
Making Connections

Theme Connection
All About Me

Vocabulary

answer	question
discussion	school
illustration	volunteer
love	

Materials

books about school (see suggestions on the right)

What to Do

- Engage the children in a discussion about what they like to do at school. To spark their thinking, show them illustrations in books about going to school (see suggestions below).
- Point to an illustration and talk about what is happening (reading, painting, and so on).
- Ask, *What is something you love to do at school?* Allow some "think time." Then ask volunteers: *(Nia), what do you love to do?*
- Record the children's answers on chart paper. Some examples might include:

> Nia: I love to hug my teacher.
> Anthony: I love to play drums.
> Shawna: I love to play hide-and-seek.

Extension Ideas

- Continue the class chart on another day.
- If your classroom is not set up to allow the children to do an activity that they like to do (playing hide-and-seek, for example), set up the room so the children can do what they love to do.

Cleo and Theo's Book Suggestions

Friends at School
by Rochelle Bunnett

Photographs and text tell the story of a diverse group of children, some with disabilities, who are friends at school.

Lissy's Friends by Grace Lin

Lissy is lonely on her first day of school, so she makes a bird from origami paper to keep her company. Soon she has a group of folded animal friends. When they blow away, a new friend comes to the rescue.

Skill Focus

Concepts of Print (Functions of Print)

Phonological Awareness (Rhythm and Repetition)

Theme Connections

All About Me

Feelings

"Birthday Chant"

What to Do

☑ Explain that everyone has a birthday. Say, *Your birthday is the day you were born. Let's look at our birthday chart and see in which month each of you were born.*

☑ Show the children the class birthday chart (see page 16). As you point to each column, recite the months of the year.

☑ Point to January. Say, *This word is* January. *January is the first month of the year. Let's see who has a birthday in January.*

☑ Say the name of each child whose name or photo appears in the *January* column. Continue the process for the remaining 11 months of the year.

☑ Ask, *Which month has the most birthdays? Are there any months with no birthdays?*

☑ Say, *Stand up if your birthday is in September.* Continue with the other months in any order.

☑ Tell the children you are going to chant a jump-rope rhyme that asks what month of the year your birthday comes.

☑ Recite the "Birthday Chant" with a bouncy rhythm.

Birthday Chant
Apples, peaches,
Pears, and plums,
Tell me when your
Birthday comes.
January, February,
March, April, May,
June, July,
August, September,
October,
November, December.

☑ Recite the chant a second time. This time, ask the children to jump up when they hear their birthday month.

Vocabulary

April	June
August	March
birthday	May
born	month
chart	name
day	November
December	October
February	September
January	stand up
July	thyme
jump rope	year

Materials

class birthday chart (see page 16)

Name Riddles

Skill Focus
Concepts of Print (Print Conveys Meaning)
Letter Formation
Letter Recognition
Vocabulary

Theme Connection
All About Me

Vocabulary

answer	hint
box	information
clue	letter
color	name
favorite	riddle
first	second
food	square
fourth	third
guess	

Materials

alphabet poster
construction paper
crayons
markers

Preparation

☐ Create a template (as shown in What to Do) for each child.

What to Do

☐ Ask the children, *Do you know what a riddle is?* Say, *A riddle is a question that you have to think about very carefully to guess the answer. A riddle gives you clues or hints to help you figure out the answer. Listen to this riddle and tell me if you can guess the answer. The riddle has four clues.*

☐ Make up and pose a simple riddle about one of the children. The riddle should have four clues that include well-known information about the child. One of the clues should be the first letter in the child's name. For example:

This child likes to play with blocks.
She is wearing a red bow.
She has a baby brother named Jackson.
Her name begins with the letter "B." (Point to the letter "Bb" on the alphabet poster and say the /b/ sound.)
Who is it?

☐ Tell the children that they will be creating riddles.
☐ Give each child a template with four boxes, as shown on the next page.

My name begins with	My favorite color is
My favorite food is	My favorite animal is

▣ Point to the words as you read each sentence aloud.

▣ Have each child complete the sentence in the first box by writing the first letter of her name. The children can complete the second, third, and fourth boxes by drawing their responses. Help the children label each drawing.

▣ Create a display of Name Riddles in a prominent place in the classroom for all to enjoy. Encourage them to guess who each riddle is about.

▣ When the children have guessed correctly, ask the child to stand up. Repeat the clues to show how each one matches the child.

Extension Idea

Gather the children around the display of name riddles. Invite them to look at and "read" one another's name riddles. Select a few to present, and invite the children to guess who they are about. Revisit the display throughout the day and week.

"Lion, Lion"

Skill Focus
Concepts of Print (Directionality)
Letter Recognition
Story Structure
Vocabulary

Theme Connections
Animals
Helping

Vocabulary

caught	lion
chart	nibble
direction	quickly
free	right
help	thank you
left to right	top
letter	word

Materials

chart paper
The Lion and the Mouse by
    Bernadette Watts, optional
markers

Click on the
*Between the
Lions* website!
pbskids.org/lions/gryphonhouse

Story: The Lion and the Mouse

Preparation

☑ Write the song "Lion, Lion" on the chart paper.

What to Do

☑ Tell the children you are going to teach them a song about *The Lion and the Mouse*. If the children are not familiar with the story, read the book to them.

☑ Display the song chart and read the title aloud. Ask the children if they can find the letter "L" in the word *Lion*.

☑ Tell the children you are going to read the words to the song. Ask, *Can anyone show me on the chart where I start reading? Yes, I start here on the top of the chart. Then I am going to read in this direction—from left to right.*

☑ Point to each word as you read aloud the first two verses of the song. Then sing the first two verses. Invite the children to sing with you. Point to each word on the chart as you sing.

Lion, Lion
(Tune: "Frère Jacques")
Lion, Lion,
Lion, Lion,
Set me free,
Set me free.
Someday I will help you.
Someday I will help you.
Set me free.
Set me free.

Little Mouse,
Little Mouse,
You can go,

You can go.
You will never help me.
You will never help me.
You're too small.
You're too small.

Lion, Lion,
Lion, Lion,
You are caught,
You are caught.
I will nibble quickly.
I will nibble quickly.
Now you're free.
Now you're free.

Little Mouse,
Little Mouse,
You were right,
You were right.
You really did help me.
You really did help me.
Thank you, Mouse.
Thank you, Mouse.

▣ After children have learned the first two verses, teach them the final two verses.

Extension Idea

Divide the class into a group of lions and a group of mice. Have the mice and the lions sing alternate verses of "Lion, Lion." Encourage the children sing the song in the Pretend and Play Center and in the Writing Center as they retell the story.

Our Favorite Colors

Skill Focus
Color Identification
Compare and Contrast
Concepts of Print (Spaces
Between Words)

Theme Connections
Colors
Counting

Vocabulary

best	less
choose	more
color	number
compare	row
count	space
favorite	square
graph	title
how many	word

Materials

chart paper
construction paper, in many
   colors
glue or tape
scissors

Click on the
*Between the
Lions* website!
pbskids.org/lions/gryphonhouse

Stories:
▣ POP POP POP POP POP
▣ Spicy Hot Colors
▣ Yesterday I Had the Blues
Poem: Yellow
Video Clip: Colorful Foods

Preparation
▣ Cut construction paper into squares that will fit the color graph
(see What to Do).

What to Do
▣ Ask the children, *What is your favorite color—the color you like
best of all?* As the children name colors, have them come to the
front of the room and choose a square of paper in that color.
▣ Have the children use their selected color squares to make a
graph.
▣ Provide a graph template like the one shown below.

Our Favorite Colors					
blue					
red					
yellow					
purple					

- Help the children glue their favorite color squares onto the graph, one by one. If a child has a new color, one that does not yet appear on the graph, start a new row. If a child has a color that already appears on the graph, help her place the square in that row, right next to the previous same-colored square.

- When all the children have placed their squares on the chart, invite them to count the number of squares in each row.

- Help the children compare the rows. Ask questions such as, *How many people like blue the best? Let's count the squares in the blue row and see. One, two! Two people like blue best. Do more people like red or yellow best? Which row has more squares? Yes, red has more squares. More people like red best.*

- Talk about words and spaces between words as you write the title "Our Favorite Colors" at the top of the chart. Say, *Let's call this graph "Our Favorite Colors." I'm going to write the first word, Our. Next I'm going to leave a space* (demonstrate) *and write the second word Favorite. Now I'm going to leave another space and write the last word, Colors.*

Cleo and Theo's Book Suggestions

The Colors of Us
by Karen Katz
A young girl mixes colors to paint pictures of her family and friends in all their different shades.

Harold and the Purple Crayon
by Crockett Johnson
This classic tale about a young boy and his crayon celebrates the imagination.

My Colors, My World/Mis Colores, Mi Mundo
by Maya Christina Gonzalez
A girl living in the desert describes the colors that remind her of the people and places she loves.

Red Is a Dragon
by Roseanne Thong
The colors that surround a young Chinese-American girl remind her of the things that she loves.

Spicy Hot Colors: Colores Picantes by Sherry Shahan
Colors explode off the page in this energetic, jazzy picture book introducing readers to colors in English and Spanish. [featured on a *Between the Lions* episode]

Yellow Elephant: A Bright Bestiary by Julie Larios
Rhyming poems describe a variety of colorful animals.

I Packed My Suitcase

Skill Focus

Concepts of Print (Directionality, Print Conveys Meaning)

Listening and Speaking (Describing)

Vocabulary

Theme Connection

Clothing

Vocabulary

baseball cap   sentence

clothing   suitcase

pack   sweater

raincoat   trip

Materials

empty suitcase

various items of clothing

What to Do

◻ Display an empty suitcase along with various items of clothing. Explain that we pack clothes into a suitcase when we go on a trip.

◻ Say, *Pretend you are going on a trip.* Ask, *What will you pack in your suitcase?*

◻ While the children watch, write the following sentences on chart paper:

I packed my suitcase. I put my _____ in it.

◻ Ask a child to choose a piece of clothing and put it into the suitcase. Ask, *What did you pack into the suitcase?* Encourage the child to name and describe the piece of clothing.

◻ Write the child's response on the chart, as shown.

Kyle: I packed my suitcase. I put my shiny, yellow raincoat in it.

Jennifer: I packed my suitcase. I put my fluffy, red sweater in it.

Barry: I packed my suitcase. I put my blue baseball cap in it.

◻ Read aloud the sentence as you point to each word.

◻ Continue with the remaining children.

Skill Focus
Concepts of Print
Name Recognition

Theme Connection
Families

Families Together

Vocabulary

chart	names
class	response
families	sentence
family	write
like to do	

Materials

chart paper
markers

What to Do

▣ Make a chart of the things the children in the class like to do with their families.

▣ Ask the children to complete the sentence: *I like to _____ with my* (family member). Encourage a wide variety of responses.

▣ Create a class chart by writing each child's response, one directly below the other, as in the example shown. Set off the children's names from the rest of the sentence by writing them in a different color.

    Brianna likes to read with her grandfather.
    Jonvante likes to cook with his father.
    Kayla likes play hide-and-seek with her brother.
    Michael likes to sing with his mother.

▣ Depending on the number of the children in your class, you may want to complete the chart over a two- or three-day period. Work with a few children each day and assure the children that everyone will have a turn.

▣ Read the chart with a small group of the children. Have each child read his sentence with you as you touch each word with a pointer.

▣ Ask each child to come up to the chart and touch his name.

Click on the
*Between the
Lions* website!
pbskids.org/lions/gryphonhouse

Video Clip: I Love My Family

"Feelings"

Skill Focus
Concepts of Print (Counting Words in Sentences, Locating Title, Spaces Between Words)
Vocabulary

Theme Connections
Feelings
Counting

Vocabulary

afternoon	mad
come	poem
fast	rainbow
feelings	rhyming
go	sad
happy	silly
highlight	slow
line	word

Materials

chart paper
markers

Click on the
Between the Lions website!
pbskids.org/lions/gryphonhouse

Stories:
- Worm Watches
- Yesterday I Had the Blues

Preparation

- Write the words to the poem "Feelings" on chart paper.

What to Do

- Point to the poem "Feelings" on chart paper.
- Say, *These are the words to a poem called "Feelings." It's about how our feelings change, how they come and go.*
- Ask a volunteer to come up to the chart and point to the title.
- Point to each word as you recite the poem.

> **Feelings**
> Feelings come and feelings go,
> Sometimes fast and sometimes slow.
> Sometimes happy, sometimes sad,
> Sometimes silly, sometimes mad.
> Feelings come and feelings go,
> Like an afternoon rainbow.

- Recite the poem again and invite the children to chime in on the rhyming words.
- After reciting, read aloud the first line, "Feelings come and feelings go," as you point to each word.
- Ask, *How many words are in this first line of the poem?* Remind the children that we make spaces between words so we know where a word begins and ends.
- Highlight each word with highlighter tape. Say, *Let's count the words. One, two, three, four, five!*

Skill Focus

Concepts of Print (Print Carries Meaning)
Listening and Speaking
Vocabulary

Theme Connections

Food

Our Favorite Foods

What to Do

▣ Tell the children about your favorite meal. Describe how it looks, tastes, and smells and whether you like to eat it for breakfast, lunch, or dinner. Say, *Show me the part of your body that you use to smell food, to taste food.*

▣ Ask, *What is your favorite food?*

▣ On a large piece of chart paper, write *What is your favorite food?* Point to the words as you read the question aloud.

▣ Write each child's response in a full sentence under the question.

> Priscilla: I like applesauce.
> Kevin: I like pizza.
> Enrique: I like ice cream.

▣ Continue for as long as the children are interested or at another time.

Cleo and Theo's Book Suggestions

Bee-bim Bop! by Linda Sue Park
In playful verse with a bouncy beat a young girl describes how her mom makes the popular Korean dish called Bee-bim bop. [featured on a *Between the Lions* episode]

Bread, Bread, Bread by Ann Morris and Ken Heyman
Simple text and color photos describe and show the different kinds of bread that people eat around the world.

Chicks & Salsa by Aaron Reynolds
The chickens at Nuthatcher Farm get tired of the same old food, so the rooster cooks up a plan for a tasty fiesta. [featured on a *Between the Lions* episode]

Pete's a Pizza by William Steig
On a rainy day, Pete's father pretends to make him into a pizza in this heartwarming and entertaining story. [featured on a *Between the Lions* episode]

Vocabulary

best	graph
breakfast	look
chart	lunch
color	row
dinner	square
eat	smell
favorite	taste
food	

Materials

chart paper
markers

Click on the
*Between the
Lions* website!
pbskids.org/lions/gryphonhouse

Stories:

▣ Bee-bim Bop!
▣ Cheesybreadville
▣ Chicks and Salsa
▣ Making Bread
▣ Stone Soup

AGE 3+

We Love Potatoes!

Skill Focus
Concepts of Print (Directionality)
Counting
Name Recognition
Vocabulary

Theme Connection
Food

Vocabulary

baked
  potatoes
catalogs
chart
columns
eat
favorite
how many
magazines

mashed
  potatoes
name
potato chips
potatoes
scalloped
  potatoes
stuffed potato

Materials

chart paper
markers
magazines or catalogs
scissors
paper
tape or glue

Preparation

☑ Cut out pictures of potatoes (baked, mashed, stuffed potato, scalloped, french fries, potato chips, and so on) from magazines or catalogs.

☑ Use paper, markers, and scissors to create a name tag for each child.

What to Do

☑ Tell the children you are going to make a chart that shows their favorite way to eat potatoes.

☑ On chart paper, create a chart with three to six columns. In each column, write the name of a way to cook potatoes (baked, mashed, stuffed potato, scalloped, french fries, potato chips, and so on). Draw or attach a picture under each name.

☑ Give each child a name tag to tape or glue under his favorite potato dish.

☑ Look at the completed chart together. Count the name tags under each potato dish. Write the sum under the last name in each column.

☑ Ask, *How many children like french fries? How many children like mashed potatoes? Do more children like baked potatoes or mashed potatoes?*

☑ Use one of the following cookbooks to make the children's favorite potato recipe.

⊡ *Children's Quick and Easy Cookbook* by Angela Wilkes
⊡ *Cook and Learn: Recipes, Songs, and Activities for Children* by Adrienne Wiland
⊡ *I'm the Chef: A Young Chef's Mexican Cookbook* by Karen Ward
⊡ *Pretend Soup and Other Real Recipes* by Mollie Katzen and Ann L. Henderson

Skill Focus
Concepts of Print (Functions of Print, Print Conveys Meaning)
Vocabulary

Theme Connection
Food

Shopping List

What to Do

◪ Engage the children in a discussion about making lists, including shopping lists.

◪ Describe some of the things you put on your shopping list. *My daughter likes cheese, so I put* cheese *on my shopping list. I am going to make chicken soup this week, so I am going to put* chicken, noodles, carrots, celery, *and* onions *on my shopping list.*

◪ Read the children a book they know and like, such as *The Lion and the Mouse*, and then have the children make shopping lists for one of the characters—the mouse or the lion—or for themselves.

◪ Talk about what the lion likes to eat (*meat*), what the mouse likes to eat (*cheese*), and what the children like to eat.

◪ The children can use a combination of scribbles, drawings, and pictures cut out of magazines or grocery store flyers to make their list.

Cleo and Theo's Book Suggestions

Bread Is for Eating
by David and Phillis Gershator and Emma Shaw-Smith
A mother sings a song to help her son appreciate the bread that he leaves on his plate. Bilingual text.

Dim Sum for Everyone! by Grace Lin
While eating dim sum at a Chinese restaurant, family members choose a favorite item from carts brought to their table.

Everybody Cooks Rice by Norah Dooley and Peter J. Thompson
A young girl discovers that all of her neighbors, despite their different backgrounds, eat rice. (See also **Everybody Brings Noodles** and **Everybody Bakes Bread** by the same author.)

Jalapeño Bagels by Natasha Wing and Robert Casilla
It's International Day at school and Pablo, whose father is Jewish and whose mother is Mexican, must decide what to bring. Includes recipes.

Vocabulary

cheese
meat
shopping list

Materials

books that the children know and like, such as *The Lion and the Mouse* by Bernadette Watts

cut-out pictures of food from magazines or grocery store flyers (including meat and cheese)

glue

writing materials

Click on the *Between the Lions* website!
pbskids.org/lions/gryphonhouse

Stories:

◪ Bee-bim Bop!
◪ Chicks and Salsa
◪ Making Bread
◪ Stone Soup

Class Poem About Food

Skill Focus
Concepts of Print
Phonological Awareness
(Rhythm, Rhyme, and
Repetition)
Word Recognition

Theme Connection
Food

Vocabulary

favorite   tamale
poem   taste
rhyme   tummy
rub   yum
substitute   yummy

Materials

markers
sentence chart
sentence strips

Click on the
*Between the
Lions* website!
pbskids.org/lions/gryphonhouse

Video Clip: Opposite Bunny:
yucky/yummy

Preparation

☐ Write each line of the poem "Yum, Yum, Yum" on sentence strips and place the strips in a sentence chart.

What to Do

☐ Tell the children that the poem "Yum, Yum, Yum" is about tamales.

☐ Recite the poem, pointing to the words as you read. Invite the children to join you. Have them rub their tummies on the last line.

> Yum, Yum, Yum
> Tamales, tamales
> Yum, yum, yum.
> Don't you wish that you had some?
> Taste so very, very yummy,
> I wish I had some in my tummy.

☐ Display the Favorite-Foods class chart (see page 161). Make new poems by substituting the children's favorite foods for the words "Tamales, tamales" in the poem "Yum, Yum, Yum."

☐ Say, *Let's change the word* tamales *in the poem to one of your favorite foods. Let's look at our Favorite-Foods chart. Kevin, Ella, Alexandra, and Liam all like pizza. So let's change the word* tamales *to the word* pizza!

☐ Point to the word *tamales* on the sentence chart. Say, *The word* tamales *is written two times in the poem. So we need to write the word* pizza *two times. Let's use the Favorite-Foods chart to help us write the word* pizza.

- Hold a blank sentence strip under the word *pizza* on the Favorite-Foods chart. Point to the first letter and ask, *What's the first letter of the word* pizza? *It's the letter "Pp." I'm going to write an uppercase "P" here because it's the first word in a sentence. What letter comes next?*
- Write the word *pizza* a second time, using a lowercase "p" at the beginning.
- Place the sentence strip with the words *Pizza, pizza* over the sentence strip with the words *Tamales, tamales* in the sentence chart. Recite the new poem, pointing to each word. Invite the children to recite the poem with you.

Extension Idea

Ask the children if they can find the letter "Tt" (*tamales, taste, tummy*) on the sentence chart of the poem. Are there any other letters the children recognize?

Cleo and Theo's Book Suggestions

Bee-bim Bop!
by Linda Sue Park
In playful verse with a bouncy beat a young girl describes how her mom makes the popular Korean dish called Bee-bim bop. [featured on a *Between the Lions* episode]

Dumpling Soup
by Jama Kim Rattigan
A Hawaiian family gathers at grandma's house to make dumplings for a New Year's celebration.

Let's Eat by Ana Zamorano
Every day Antonio's mother tries to get everyone to sit down together to eat, but someone is always busy elsewhere.

Mama Provi and the Pot of Rice by Sylvia Rosa-Casanova
Mama Provi makes *arroz con pollo* for her granddaughter, who has the chicken pox.

Tortillas and Lullabies/ Tortillas y cancioncitas
by Lynn Reiser
Large colorful paintings show three generations sharing family traditions, including making tortillas.

Where Does Food Come From?
by Shelley Rotner and Gary Goss
Photographs and text show the natural source of many of the foods children enjoy.

AGE 4+

Give a Friend a Cheer!

Skill Focus
Concepts of Print (Directionality, Print Conveys Meaning, Punctuation, Return Sweep)
Word Recognition

Theme Connections
Friends
Helping

Vocabulary

best	song
cheer	three
four	title
friend	two
fun	word
happy	yes
one	

Materials

chart paper
markers

Click on the *Between the Lions* website!
pbskids.org/lions/gryphonhouse

Stories:

- ☒ Owen and Mzee
- ☒ Yo! Yes?

Preparation

☒ Write the song "Yo! Yes! Do Your Best!" on chart paper.

What to Do

☒ Sing the first verse of "Yo! Yes! Do Your Best!" to the children but don't display the song chart.

Yo! Yes! Do Your Best!
(*Tune: "This Old Man"*)
This good friend,
She said one. (*Hold up one finger.*)
She said, "Come, let's have some fun."
With a Yo! Yes! Do your best,
Give a friend a cheer.
We are happy you are here.

This good friend,
He said two. (*Hold up two fingers.*)
He said, "Can I play with you?"
With a Yo! Yes! Do your best,
Give a friend a cheer.
We are happy you are here.

This good friend,
She said three. (*Hold up three fingers.*)
She said, "Will you play with me?"
With a Yo! Yes! Do your best,
Give a friend a cheer.
We are happy you are here.

This good friend,
He said four. (*Hold up four fingers.*)
He said, "Can we play some more?"
With a Yo! Yes! Do your best,
Give a friend a cheer.
We are happy you are here.
Hip! Hip! Hooray! (*Children cheer.*)

▣ Invite the children to join you as you sing the second, third, and fourth verses.

▣ Display the "Yo! Yes! Do Your Best!" song on chart paper. Point to the words as you read the title aloud. Say, *These are the words to a song.*

▣ Ask a volunteer to come up to the chart and point to the words *Yo* and *Yes* in the title. Point to the exclamation points after each of the words and ask, *What is this? Is this a letter? No, it's an exclamation point. Let's say the title "Yo! Yes! Do Your Best!" in our most excited voices.*

▣ Sing the first two verses of the song with the children. As you sing, move your finger under the words, exaggerating slightly the return sweep of your hand to the beginning of the next line.

▣ Sing all four verses of the song together.

Extension Idea

Ask the children to point out any other letters that they recognize on the song chart.

Cleo and Theo's Book Suggestions

Bein' with You This Way
by W. Nikola-Lisa
A group of children playing together in the park celebrate their differences. [adapted for a *Between the Lions* episode]

Earl's Too Cool for Me
by Leah Komaiko and Laura Cornell
Even though Earl is so cool that he "taught an octopus how to scrub," he's willing to make new friends. [featured on a *Between the Lions* episode]

How to Lose All Your Friends by Nancy Carlson
This book tells what to do to make sure that you don't have any friends. In the process, children learn positive behaviors that help them make and get along with friends.

Matthew and Tilly
by Rebecca C. Jones
After best friends Matthew and Tilly argue over a broken crayon, they apologize and find a way to be friends again.

We Are Best Friends by Aliki
When a boy's best friend moves away, he learns that he can make new friends and still be loyal to his best one.

Listening Walk

Skill Focus
Concepts of Print (Directionality, Print Conveys Meaning, Spaces Between Words)
Letter Recognition

Theme Connections
My Neighborhood
Sounds

Vocabulary

describe	responses
hear	sound
listen	walk
notebook	write
playground	

Materials

chart paper
markers
notebook
pen

What to Do

- Take the children on a listening walk around the playground or in your neighborhood.
- Pause occasionally to stop and listen quietly. Ask, *What do you hear? What is making that sound? Do you hear anything else?*
- In a notebook, write down the different sounds the children name and describe.
- When you return to the classroom, invite the children to write about what they heard on the listening walk.
- On chart paper, write a heading and an opening line (see example). Ask each child to name and describe a sound that she heard. Encourage a variety of responses. Refer to your notebook to remind children of the different sounds they heard. List each child's response next to her name, as shown.

Sounds All Around

We went on a listening walk. We heard

Kaitlen: a dog bark
Max: a train whistle
Sienna: a baby crying

- As you write, talk about where you start each line, how you form the letters, and the spaces you leave between words. Point to each word as you read aloud the completed chart.
- Invite each child to read her entry with you.

Click on the *Between the Lions* website!
pbskids.org/lions/gryphonhouse

Song: Very Loud, Very Big, Very Metal

Skill Focus
Concepts of Print
Letter Recognition
Vocabulary
Word Recognition

Theme Connections
Nighttime
Stars

"Twinkle, Twinkle, Little Star"

Preparation
◻ Write the song "Twinkle, Twinkle, Little Star" on chart paper.
◻ Write the word *stars* on a blank index card.

What to Do
◻ Display the "Twinkle, Twinkle, Little Star" song on chart paper. Point to the words as you read aloud the title.

Twinkle, Twinkle, Little Star
Twinkle, twinkle, little star, (*Open and close fingers as you say each word.*)
How I wonder what you are! (*Look up and tap head with a finger.*)
Up above the world so high, (*Reach up to the sky.*)
Like a diamond in the sky. (*Make a diamond shape with hands.*)
Twinkle, twinkle, little star, (*Open and close fingers as you say each word.*)
How I wonder what you are! (*Look up and tap head with a finger.*)

◻ Hold up the *stars* word card. Say the word with the children.
◻ Point to the first letter and ask, *What is the first letter in the word* stars? Point to and name each letter. Point to the final letter "s" and ask, *What is the last letter in the word* stars?
◻ Cover the final letter "s." Say, *When we take away the last letter "s" in the word* stars, *we have the word* star. *That means there is only one star.*
◻ Recite "Twinkle, Twinkle, Little Star" with the motions.
◻ Point to each word as you recite the poem a second time. Pause when you point to the word *star* in the first and fifth lines and have the children say the word.

Vocabulary

diamond	star
high	twinkle
letter	wonder
little	word
sky	world

Materials

blank index cards
chart paper
markers

Click on the
*Between the
Lions* website!
pbskids.org/lions/gryphonhouse

Song: Mighty Star Lion

"Night Music"

Skill Focus
Concepts of Print (Counting Words in a Title, Directionality, Return Sweep)
Word Recognition

Theme Connections
Sounds
Nighttime

Vocabulary

breeze · music
chant · noises
country · slowly
frogs · sounds
imagine · whisper
listen

Materials

chart paper
markers

Click on the *Between the Lions* website!
pbskids.org/lions/gryphonhouse

Story: Night in the Country

Preparation

☒ Write the poem "Night Music" on chart paper.

What to Do

☒ Tell the children to imagine it is nighttime in the country.

☒ You may wish to darken the room and ask the children to close their eyes as you recite "Night Music." Read slowly in a hushed tone.

Night Music

Night in the country,
Listen to the sounds.
Night in the country,
There are noises all around.

Night in the country,
Listen to the sounds.
Night in the country,
There's music all around.

Listen to the wind,
Whispering through the
    trees.
Listen to the frogs,
Chanting in the breeze.

☒ After reading the poem, ask, *What noises did you hear in the poem? What made the noises?*

☒ Explain that when we whisper, we speak very softly. *When the wind whispers, it makes a soft hissing sound.* Demonstrate the sound by blowing air out through your lips.

☒ Display the "Night Music" poem on chart paper. Tell the children these are the words to the poem you just read. Read the poem a second time. Move your finger under the words, exaggerating slightly the return sweep of your hand to the beginning of the next line. Talk to the children about why the poem is called "Night Music." Explain that sometimes night noises sound beautiful, just like music.

Skill Focus

Concepts of Print (Directionality, Return Sweep)
Letter Recognition
Phonological Awareness (Beginning Sounds)

Theme Connection

Sounds

"Peter Piper Paints"

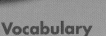

AGE 4+

Preparation

◻ Write the poem "Peter Piper Paints" on chart paper

What to Do

◻ Display the "Peter Piper Paints" poem chart at the children's eye level. Tell the children that these are the words to the poem.

◻ Point to the words as you read aloud the title. Ask, *How many words are in the title?* Let a volunteer come up and count. Ask, *What else do you notice about the title?* (Each of the words begins with the letter "P.")

◻ Recite "Peter Piper Paints," emphasizing the /p/ sound at the beginning of the words. Repeat the first sentence and ask, *What sound do you hear at the beginning of* Peter, Piper, paints, picture, *and* penguin? Have the children listen to the next sentence of the poem and identify one more word that starts with the /p/ sound (*pie*). Repeat with the third and fourth sentences (*polka-dot, potato, pink, purple*).

Peter Piper Paints
Peter Piper paints
a picture of a penguin.
Peter Piper paints
a picture of a pie.
Peter Piper paints
a polka-dot potato.
Peter Piper paints
a pink-and-purple sky.

Vocabulary

beginning	poem
first	polka dot
paint	potato
penguin	purple
pie	sky
pink	sound

Materials

chart paper
markers

■ Read the first two lines again, tracing your finger under the words and exaggerating slightly the return sweep of your hand to the beginning of the second line. Ask, *When I reached the end of the first line, where did my hand go? Show me. Yes, when I came to the end of the line, I went back to the beginning of the next line and kept on reading.*

■ Have the children chant the first two lines with you as you point to the words. Continue reading the rhyme together. Pause several more times at the end of a line to ask, *Where should my hand go next?*

Extension Ideas

■ Place a blank piece of paper over the last word in each sentence (*penguin, pie, potato, sky*). Tell the children that they will write their own version of the poem by having Peter Piper paint four new things beginning with the /p/ sound.

■ Display labeled pictures the children have made for *Pictionary* (see page 180), or display labeled pictures of animals and food items beginning with the letter "P" and the /p/ sound. Repeat the words with the children.

■ Read "Peter Piper Paints" together, stopping at the end of each line for the children to choose a /p/ picture word to insert. Then point to the words as you read the new poem with the four new picture words.

Click on the
Between the Lions website!
pbskids.org/lions/gryphonhouse

Story: Worm Paints

Video Clips:

■ Choppers Chop, Shoppers Shop

■ This is the sixth sister.

Game: Theo's Puzzles

Chapter 7

Alphabet Knowledge and Letter Recognition

In this chapter of *Wild About Literacy*, name games, word walls, word cards, and alphabet, song, and poem charts help children recognize letters in familiar words and associate the names of letters with their shapes and sounds, essential literacy skills (see The Literacy Scope and Sequence on pages 14–15). Tactile letter shaping, letter sorting, writing, art, and movement activities offer multiple ways for children to learn how to form letters.

The activities in this chapter are grouped alphabetically by topic and then by age (3+ or 4+) within each topic or theme. The activities have the following components:

Skill Focus	Materials
Theme Connection(s)	Preparation (if necessary)
Vocabulary	What to Do

Skill Focus—lists the literacy skills that the activity addresses and other skills that young children need to learn, such as fine motor skills or emotional awareness.

Theme Connections—lists one or two familiar early childhood themes that the activity covers. If more than one theme is listed, the first is the one with the strongest connection.

Vocabulary—lists words that are part of the activity. Use these when you are engaging children in the activity, defining their meaning if necessary. Repeat these words throughout the day so children hear the words used in context and can begin to understand how each word is used.

Materials—lists, in alphabetical order, the materials you will need to do the activity. Be sure you have the materials you need before you begin the activity.

A Note About Repetition: You will find the same songs, poems, and books used in multiple activities in *Wild About Literacy*. Children benefit and learn from repetition. When children hear a familiar song or poem, they may learn something new or solidify what they already know. Using a familiar song or story to teach a new skill is a technique used by many teachers, which is why you will find repetition in this book.

Preparation—If the activity needs any preparation, such as writing a song or poem on chart paper or preparing a chart, what you need to do is described in this section.

What to Do—Step by step, this section outlines how to engage children in the activity.

In addition, many activities include ideas that build on the main activity, extend it to another curriculum area, or suggest books that relate to the activity.

The following children's books are used in two activities in this chapter:
It Begins with an A by Stephanie Calmenson (see page 176)
The Letters Are Lost! by Lisa Campbell Ernst (see page 177)

In addition, many children's books are suggested as a way to extend an activity. Some of the book suggestions in this chapter include:
Alphabet Mystery by Audrey Wood and Bruce Wood
The Hidden Alphabet by Laura Vaccaro Seeger
K Is for Kiss Good Night by Jill Sardegna
Q Is for Duck: An Alphabet Guessing Game by Michael Folsom, Mary Elting, and Jack Kent
The Turn-Around, Upside-Down Alphabet Book by Lisa Campbell Ernst

Click on the *Between the Lions* website!
pbskids.org/lions/gryphonhouse

Books About Reading
Books Featured on *Between the Lions*
Recommended Books

"ABC Song"

What to Do

◻ Point to each letter on an alphabet chart as you sing the "ABC Song" with the children.

A-B-C-D-E-F-G
H-I-J-K-L-M-N-O-P
Q-R-S
T-U-V
W-X-Y and Z
Now I know my ABCs,
Next time won't you sing with me?

◻ Try singing the song to a different tune and rhythm. For example, sing the song to the tune of "99 Bottles of Beer on the Wall."

◻ Clap twice after the letter "M" and after the letter "Z." (Clapping and pausing after the letter "M" will break up the sounds of "L, M, N, O, P" and help the children recognize them as separate letters.)

Extension Idea

In chalk, write the uppercase letters of the alphabet clockwise in a big circle on the ground. Sing "Here We Go 'Round the Alphabet." Then, one by one, have each child walk around the circle, stopping at each letter and saying its name.

Here We Go Round the Alphabet
(Tune: "Here We Go 'Round the Mulberry Bush")
Here we go round the alphabet, the alphabet,
  the alphabet.
Here we go round the alphabet,
From A to Z we go.

Vocabulary

alphabet	rhythm
chart	sing
clap	song
letter	sound
pause	tune

Materials

alphabet chart

Click on the
*Between the
Lions* website!
pbskids.org/lions/gryphonhouse

Song: Library A to Z
Game: ABCD Watermelon

It Begins with an A

Skill Focus
Alphabet Awareness
Letter Recognition
Vocabulary

Theme Connections
Alphabet
Animals
Sounds

Vocabulary

airplane	pillow
answer	quarter
camera	question
giraffe	rabbit
hammer	riddle
icing	spaghetti
jar	tail
kangaroo	umbrella
lollipop	x-ray
moon	zebra
owl	

Materials

It Begins with an A by Stephanie Calmenson

Click on the *Between the Lions* website!
pbskids.org/lions/gryphonhouse

Games:
- Fuzzy Lion Ears
- Theo's Puzzles

What to Do

- Read aloud *It Begins with an A* to individuals or small groups.
- Point to each box as you read the corresponding words.
- Trace each uppercase letter.
- Point to each word as you read the question WHAT IS IT? at the end of each page.
- Pause to allow the children to guess the answer to each riddle. Show the children the last two pages in the book that provide the answers to the riddles.
- Point to each letter with the accompanying illustration and together say the letter and the word: "A"—*airplane*.

Cleo and Theo's Book Suggestions

Alphabet Mystery by Audrey Wood and Bruce Wood
When little "x" goes missing, the other letters of the alphabet set out to find him. (Also see ***Alphabet Adventure*** by the same author.)

The Hidden Alphabet by Laura Vaccaro Seeger
Alphabet letters are hidden in bold graphic images.

K Is for Kiss Good Night by Jill Sardegna
Diverse families tell about their special bedtime routines in this comforting alphabet book. (Look for this out-of-print title in libraries.)

Q Is for Duck: An Alphabet Guessing Game
by Michael Folsom, Mary Elting, and Jack Kent
Children learn the sounds that animals make and the sounds that letters make in this clever book of alphabet riddles.

The Turn-Around, Upside-Down Alphabet Book
by Lisa Campbell Ernst
In this unusual alphabet book, each letter becomes three different objects when you turn the book in different directions.

Skill Focus
Alphabet Awareness
Letter Recognition
Vocabulary

Theme Connection
Alphabet

The Letters Are Lost!

What to Do

◪ Read aloud *The Letters Are Lost!* to individual children or small groups.

◪ Encourage the children to touch the letter blocks on each page as you read them aloud.

◪ Have the children name some of the items on the page that begin with the featured letter. For example, ask, *Where is the letter "A"? Yes, it's in the airplane! Airplane begins with the letter "A."*

◪ Ask the children to tell you when you get to the page that features the first letter in their name. Explain the meaning of unfamiliar words, such as *disappeared, empty, jig, oval, peeked, quilt, squish, upside down,* and *xylophone.*

Extension Idea

Give one child a xylophone. Ask this child to play the xylophone when you read that word, when you say a certain letter of the alphabet (the first letter in his name), or another word or letter in the book.

Vocabulary

alphabet	lost
alphabet book	oval
disappeared	peeked
empty	quilt
jack-in-the-	squish
box	upside down
jig	xylophone
letter	

Materials

The Letters Are Lost! by Lisa Campbell Ernst

Click on the
Between the Lions website!
pbskids.org/lions/gryphonhouse

Games:
◪ Monkey Match
◪ Sky Riding

Letter Hunt

Vocabulary

alphabet	disappear
alphabetical order	find
	hunt
chart	letter
clipboard	lost

Materials

alphabet chart
clipboard, paper, and pen
wooden alphabet blocks or
   plastic letters

Click on the
Between the Lions website!
pbskids.org/lions/gryphonhouse

Games:

- ⊠ Monkey Match
- ⊠ Sky Riding
- ⊠ Theo's Puzzles

Preparation

⊠ Before the children arrive, hide the first six letters of the alphabet around the room. Use wooden alphabet blocks or plastic letters. (You may want to place letters on or near an object that begins with the same letter. For instance, "A" can be in the Art Center and "B" can be on top of a book.)

What to Do

⊠ Have the children go on a letter hunt to find the "lost" letters in your classroom.

⊠ Gather the children around the alphabet chart. Explain that a strange thing has happened. You had some letters on the bookcase this morning and some of them have disappeared.

⊠ Point to the first six letters on the alphabet chart and ask the children to say them with you. These are the letters that are lost.

⊠ Ask the children to go on a hunt to find the lost letters. When a child finds a letter, instruct the child to stand next to the letter and raise her hand. Collect the letter from the child and, on a clipboard, record the name of the letter, who found the letter, and where it was found.

⊠ At the end of the hunt, hold up the "found" letters in alphabetical order. Ask, *Who found the letter "A"?* Give the letter to the child and ask where she found it. After all the letters are located, congratulate the children for finding the lost letters.

Extension Idea

Repeat this activity on another day with six more letters. Repeat on subsequent days until the children find all the letters of the alphabet.

Skill Focus
Alphabet Awareness
Phonological Awareness (Rhythm and Repetition)

Theme Connection
Alphabet

Where Can the Alphabet Be?

What to Do

▣ Before singing the song, talk with the children about the alphabet.

▣ Sing the song once. As you sing, point to the letters "A" through "Z" on the alphabet chart.

Oh Where, Oh Where Has the Alphabet Gone?
(*Tune: "Oh, Where, Oh, Where Has My Little Dog Gone?"*)
Oh, where, oh, where has the alphabet gone?
Oh, where, oh, where can it be?
With 26 letters from A to Z,
Oh, where, oh, where can it be?

▣ Invite the children to sing along with you.

Extension Idea

Challenge the children to look around and find the letters of the alphabet on signs and charts in the classroom.

Vocabulary

alphabet   letters
chart   where

Materials

alphabet chart

Click on the *Between the Lions* website!
pbskids.org/lions/gryphonhouse

Song: Library A to Z
Games:
▣ ABCD Watermelon
▣ Sky Riding

Pictionary

Skill Focus
Letter Recognition
Letter-Sound Correspondence
Phonological Awareness
(Beginning Sounds)

Theme Connection
Alphabet

Vocabulary

begin	page
dictionary	picture
first letter	sound
label	word

Materials

crayons, markers, pencils
glue
large sheets of paper
objects (or pictures of objects)
   beginning with the letter "D"
   (dog, doll, drum, dump truck,
   dragon, duck, donut)
simple picture dictionary
squares of drawing paper

Click on the
*Between the
Lions* website!
pbskids.org/lions/gryphonhouse

Song: Dixie Chimps: Delighted
   You're Mine

Games:
- Fuzzy Lion Ears
- Monkey Match (beginning
   sounds)
- Theo's Puzzles

What to Do

- Show the children a very simple picture dictionary.
  Note: You can use this approach for any letter of the alphabet.
  For this activity, the letter "Dd" is used.
- Turn the pages, noting that the pictures on the first pages all
  begin with "Aa," "Bb," and then "Cc."
- Stop at the "Dd" page, and name some of the words with the
  children.
- Point to the first letter in a picture label and ask, *What's the first
  letter in the word?* Repeat with other picture labels, helping the
  children realize that all the words on that page begin with the
  letter "Dd" and the /d/ sound.
- Have the children help you gather classroom objects (or pictures
  of objects) that begin with the /d/ sound.
- Write a label for each object on a small square of drawing paper
  and place the squares of paper and the objects in a "Dd" display
  in the classroom.
- Have the children draw a picture of an object in the "Dd"
  display and help them write the word below the picture.

Extension Idea

Have the children create a picture for one or more letters of the
alphabet. Sort the labeled drawings, grouping pictures of the same
letter together. Make a class big book, *Pictionary*. Glue or tape the
pictures to the pages, writing the word label in large letters for
each group of pictures. Alphabetize the words and feature one or
two words per page. Assemble the class big book, *Pictionary*, with
the children. Read it aloud together.

Beginning Writing Together

The activities in this chaper of *Wild About Literacy*, motivate children to learn to write when they discover that what they think and say can be written down and read by others (see The Literacy Scope and Sequence on pages 14–15). They learn to write by observing others write. Provide many instances for the children to see you writing, such as when writing information on class charts, in addition to providing many opportunities for children to write or respond to stories by drawing, scribbling, or dictating their stories, thoughts, and ideas.

The activities in this chapter are grouped alphabetically by topic and then by age (3+ or 4+) within each topic or theme. The activities have the following components:

Skill Focus	**Materials**
Theme Connection(s)	**Preparation (if necessary)**
Vocabulary	**What to Do**

Skill Focus—lists the literacy skills that the activity addresses and other skills that young children need to learn, such as fine motor skills or emotional awareness.

Theme Connections—lists one or two familiar early childhood themes that the activity covers. If more than one theme is listed, the first is the one with the strongest connection.

Vocabulary—lists words that are part of the activity. Use these when you are engaging children in the activity, defining their meaning if necessary. Repeat these words throughout the day so children hear the words used in context and can begin to understand how each word is used.

Materials—lists, in alphabetical order, the materials you will need to do the activity. Be sure you have the materials you need before you begin the activity.

Preparation—If the activity needs any preparation, such as writing a song or poem on chart paper or preparing a chart, what you need to do is described in this section.

A Note About Repetition: You will find the same songs, poems, and books used in multiple activities in *Wild About Literacy*. Children benefit and learn from repetition. When children hear a familiar song or poem, they may learn something new or solidify what they already know. Using a familiar song or story to teach a new skill is a technique used by many teachers, which is why you will find repetition in this book.

What to Do—Step by step, this section outlines how to engage children in the activity.

In addition, many activities include ideas that build on the main activity, extend it to another curriculum area, or suggest books that relate to the activity.

Many children's books are suggested as a way to extend one or more activities in this chapter. Some of the book suggestions in this chapter include:

Being Friends by Karen Beaumont and Joy allen
Coyote Places the Stars by Harriet Peck Taylor
How the Stars Fell into the Sky: A Navajo Legend
    by Jerrie Oughton and Lisa Desmini
How to Lose All Your Friends by Nancy Carlson
I Am a Star by Jean Marzollo and Judith Moffatt
A Kid's Best Friend by Maya Ajmera and Alex Fisher
Lissy's Friends by Grace Lin
My Friend Isabelle by Eliza Woloson and Bryan Gough
Our Stars by Anne Rockwell
Spicy Hot Colors: Colores Picantes
    by Sherry Shahan and Paula Barragan [featured on a *Between the Lions* episode]
Star Blanket by Pat Brisson and Erica Magnus
The Star People: A Lakota Story by S. D. Nelson
Stargazers by Gail Gibbons
Stars by Steve Tomecek
Walter Was Worried by Laura Vaccaro Seeger
We Are Best Friends by Aliki
Yesterday I Had the Blues
    by Jeron Ashford Frame and R. Gregory Christie [featured on a *Between the Lions* episode]

Click on the *Between the Lions* website!
pbskids.org/lions/gryphonhouse

Books About Reading
Books Featured on *Between the Lions*
Recommended Books
Song: Got a Good Reason to Write

Theme Connection
All About Me

Name Collages

AGE
4+

Preparation

☑ Help the children cut out letters from magazines and newspapers. As they cut out letters, help them name the letters.

What to Do

☑ Display cut-out letters and show the children how to make a name collage by selecting the letters of their names and pasting them, in order, onto a piece of construction paper.

☑ Use markers or crayons to write their names on their papers.

☑ Help the children select the letters in their names and create their name collage.

Extension Idea

Suggest that the children use pictures from magazines, newspapers, and catalogs to make collages about their friends or any topic that interests them.

Vocabulary

collage	magazine
in order	newspaper
letter	uppercase
lowercase	

Materials

construction paper
glue or paste
magazines, newspapers, and catalogs
markers or crayons
scissors

My T-Shirt Says...

Skill Focus
Concepts of Print (Print Conveys
Meaning, Spaces Between Words)
Creative Expression
Early Writing

Theme Connections
All About Me
Clothing

Vocabulary

letters   T-shirt
message   writing

Materials

clothesline
clothespins
construction paper
crayons
markers
pencils
scissors
T-shirts with writing on the front

Preparation

☒ Cut out a construction-paper T-shirt for each child.

What to Do

☒ Display a few T-shirts with writing on the front. Talk about the writing and design on the shirts (and on any T-shirts the children may be wearing).

☒ Give each child a piece of construction paper cut into the shape of a T-shirt.

☒ Invite the children to illustrate and write words on their T-shirts.

☒ Some children may want to dictate and have you write their words. Talk about each letter as you write, and point out the spaces you leave between words.

☒ Hang the T-shirts on a clothesline for all to see.

Extension Idea

Ask each child to read or talk about her T-shirt.

Skill Focus
Book Appreciation
Concepts of Print
Creative Expression
Early Writing

Theme Connection
All About Me

Our Favorite Books

What to Do

- Have the children think of a favorite book or a favorite kind of book.
- Ask them to draw something they like about the book.
- Write the title of the book on the drawing. Think aloud as you write the letters in the title: *Your favorite book is* Owl Babies. *I like* Owl Babies, *too! I'm going to start by writing the word* Owl *here on your picture. Then I'll write the word* Babies.
- Help the children write their name on their drawings.

Extension Idea
Create an "Our Favorite Books" bulletin board.

Vocabulary

book	think
draw	title
drawing	word
favorite	write
names	

Materials

crayons
drawing paper
markers

Click on the
*Between the
Lions* website!
pbskids.org/lions/gryphonhouse

Song: Read a Book Today!

"I Can" Class Book

Skill Focus
Concepts of Print
Dictating Sentences
Writing Name

Theme Connection
All About Me

Vocabulary

accordion	sentence
book	side by side
caption	trace
display	write
name	words
read	

Materials

markers and/or crayons

pencils

square pieces of drawing paper

tape

What to Do

▣ Have each child draw a picture of something he can do.

▣ Ask each child to dictate a caption for the picture by completing the sentence: I can _____. Write the child's sentence under the picture.

▣ Point to the words as you read the sentence aloud with the child. If the child wishes, he or she can trace over the words.

▣ Ask the child to write his or her name on the page.

▣ Tape all the pages together, side by side, and display on the wall for the class to "read" together.

▣ Afterward, you can fold the pages into an accordion book (fold on the tape).

▣ Together, brainstorm a title for the class book and create a cover. Place it in the Library Center for the children to read and enjoy.

Skill Focus
Concepts of Print
Dictating Sentences
Writing Name

Theme Connections
All About Me
Food
Friends

Our Class Bakes Cookies

AGE
4+

What to Do

- Tell the children that they are going to create a book called "Our Class Bakes Cookies."
- Each child will contribute a page to the book. Brainstorm with the children a list of ingredients they might like to put in their cookies, such as flour, eggs, chocolate chips, walnuts, sugar, and so on.
- Have each child complete the sentence:

  (Child's name) puts (ingredient) into the bowl.

- Write each child's sentence on a piece of construction paper. The child can write her name, and you can complete the sentence as she dictates.
- Think aloud as you write, pointing out the beginning and end of each word and the spaces between the words.
- Ask each child to illustrate her page.
- Create a cover.
- Use a stapler to bind the pages together to make a class book. Cover the staples with duct tape for added durability and safety.
- Read the book to the children.
- If possible, laminate the book and then put it in the Library Center for the children to read.

Extension Idea

Ask each child to read her page to the class or to you.

Vocabulary

bake	flour
between	ingredients
book	sentence
butter	spaces
cover	sugar
create	words
dictate	write

Materials

construction paper
crayons
duct tape
markers
stapler

Click on the *Between the Lions* website!
pbskids.org/lions/gryphonhouse

Stories:
- Edna Bakes Cookies
- Making Bread

Family Fun Stories

Skill Focus
Concepts of Print
Creative Expression
Early Writing

Theme Connection
Families

Vocabulary

book
brother
family
father
frame
grandma
grandpa
illustration
mother
photographs
sister

Materials

books about families (see pages 201–202)
colored paper
crayons
family photos
glue
markers
scissors

What to Do

☑ Show the children books about families. Point to one of the illustrations or photos in one of the books and ask the children to talk about it. *Yes, this is a picture of a mom and dad taking a walk with their baby. Where do you think they are going?*

☑ Have the children draw a picture of their family doing something fun together, or ask the children to talk about and describe a family photo.

☑ Use colored paper to make a frame for the picture or photo.

Extension Idea

Ask the children to tell you the names of the people in their pictures and what is happening. Write the words in a caption on the bottom of the picture frame. Point to each word as you read aloud the caption. Help the children write their names on their pictures. Hang the framed pictures around the classroom.

Click on the *Between the Lions* website!
pbskids.org/lions/gryphonhouse

Story: My Dog Is As Smelly As Dirty Socks
Game: I Love My Family

Skill Focus

Concepts of Print (Directionality, Print Conveys Meaning)
Dictating Sentences
Emotional Awareness
Vocabulary

Theme Connection

Feelings

Feelings Book

What to Do

* Tell the children that the class is going to write a book about feelings.

Feeling Happy

* Say, *Every day we are going to write about a different feeling. Today we are going to write a page about feeling happy.*
* Before beginning to write the book, ask the children to choose a color marker for you to write with. Ask, *What color makes you feel happy?*
* Write the words *Happy is* at the top of the page.
* Ask the children to name things that make them feel happy. Write their responses below the heading as shown.

Happy is

an ice-cream cone with sprinkles on top.
a hug from Mom.
playing with my big brother.

* If the children remain interested, create a new page for *excited, sad,* or *silly.*

Feeling Disappointed

* On the same or another day, write a new page in the class book about feeling disappointed.
* Have the children choose a new color marker for you to use.
* If there is time, you may also want to create a page about another feeling.

Vocabulary

angry	frustrated
book	happy
color	responses
different	sad
disappointed	silly
excited	thankful
feel	write
feeling	

Materials

markers
paper

Click on the *Between the Lions* website!
pbskids.org/lions/gryphonhouse

Stories:
* Worm Watches
* Yesterday I Had the Blues

Feeling Frustrated

- On the same day or another day, write a new page in the class book about feeling frustrated.
- Have the children choose a new color marker for you to use.
- If there is time, you may also want to create a page about another feeling.

Feeling Angry

- On the same day or another day, write a new page in the class book about feeling angry.
- Have the children choose a new color marker for you to use.
- If there is time, you may also want to create a page about another feeling.

Feeling Thankful

- On the same day or another day, write a new page in the class book about feeling thankful.
- Have the children choose a new color marker for you to use.
- If there is time, you may also want to make a page for another feeling.

Extension Idea

Read aloud the completed book. Together decide on a title for the book. Make a cover. You may want to illustrate the cover and pages of the book with photographs of the children showing the different emotions. Bind the book and display it in the Library Center for the children to read and enjoy.

Skill Focus

Concepts of Print (Functions of Print, Print Conveys Meaning)
Dictating Sentences
Vocabulary

Theme Connections

Feelings
Friends

Greeting Card

What to Do

- Ask the children to think of someone they really care about. Ask, *How do you feel about your special person? What makes your special person happy? What would you like to tell your special person?*
- Invite the children to draw and write a card for their special person.
- Before the children begin to draw and write the card, you may want to show them some commercial or homemade greeting cards. Talk about the words and pictures and point out the front, the two inside pages, and the back of the cards.
- Give each child a folded piece of paper. Act as a scribe and write the child's message on the card.
- As you write, talk about the letters and the spaces you leave between words. Point to the words as you read them aloud.
- Have the children illustrate their cards and sign their names.
- Talk with the children about how they will deliver their cards.

Vocabulary

back	happy
card	inside
dear	love
from	message to
front	

Materials

commercial or homemade
   greeting cards
crayons
drawing paper
markers

4+

AGE

Feelings

Skill Focus
Concepts of Print
Interpreting Illustrations
Social and Emotional Awareness
Vocabulary
Word Recognition

Theme Connection
Feelings

Vocabulary

arms	happy
circle	lonely
excited	mouth
exclamation mark	question
	question mark
expression	sad
face	shy
hands	tone of voice

Materials

books about feelings (see list on the right)

writing materials

Click on the *Between the Lions* website! pbskids.org/lions/gryphonhouse

Stories:

☒ Worm Watches

☒ Yesterday I Had the Blues

What to Do

☒ Read aloud a book about feelings to individuals or small groups.

☒ As you read each page, say, *Look at the boy's (girl's) face. Look at his body.* Ask, *What do you think he is feeling? What could he be thinking?*

☒ Point out the punctuation that the author uses in the book. Explain that when we write a question, we put a question mark at the end. Explain that an exclamation point means that the character is saying something in a loud or excited voice.

☒ Invite the children to say a sentence from one of the books, such as *Yo! Yes?* by Chris Raschka. Prompt them to change the tone of their voices depending on whether the word is followed by a question mark or an exclamation point.

Cleo and Theo's Book Suggestions

Lots of Feelings by Shelley Rotner
Color photographs of children and simple text introduce a range of emotions.

Spicy Hot Colors: Colores Picantes by Sherry Shahan
Colors explode off the page in this energetic, jazzy picture book introducing readers to colors in English and Spanish. [featured on a *Between the Lions* episode]

Today I Feel Silly & Other Moods That Make My Day
by Jamie Lee Curtis and Laura Cornell
Young readers identify and explore their many emotions as they read about a young girl whose mood changes from silly to angry to excited.

Walter Was Worried by Laura Vaccaro Seeger
This alphabet book explores children's emotional reactions to a storm.

Skill Focus
Concepts of Print (Print Conveys Meaning, Spaces Between Words)
Dictating Sentences
Vocabulary

Theme Connection
Friends

Friends-Together Class Chart

What to Do

☑ Ask the children, *What do you like to do with your friends?* Encourage a wide variety of responses.

☑ On chart paper, record the children's responses to the question *What do you like to do with your friends?* as shown.

☑ As you write, talk about how you form the letters in the children's names and in the repeating words.

☑ Point out the spaces that you leave between words.

> Nicholas: I like to play blocks with my friends.
> Julia: I like to sing songs with my friends.
> Curtis: I like to read books with my friends.

☑ Continue until you have recorded a response for each child. It may take more than one day to complete the chart.

Cleo and Theo's Book Suggestions

Being Friends by Karen Beaumont and Joy allen
Despite their differences, two girls know that the key to friendship is having one special thing in common: they like being friends.

Earl's Too Cool for Me by Leah Komaiko and Laura Cornell
Even though Earl is so cool that he "taught an octopus how to scrub," he's willing to make new friends. [featured on a *Between the Lions* episode]

Friends at School by Rochelle Bunnett and Matt Brown
Photographs and text tell the story of a diverse group of children, some with disabilities, who are friends at school.

How to Lose All Your Friends by Nancy Carlson
This book tells what to do to make sure that you don't have any friends. In the process, children learn positive behaviors that help them make and get along with friends.

Vocabulary

chart	record
friends	responses
letter	spaces
like to do	words

Materials

chart paper
markers

Click on the *Between the Lions* website!
pbskids.org/lions/gryphonhouse

Stories:
☑ Owen and Mzee
☑ Yo! Yes?

A Kid's Best Friend by Maya Ajmera and Alex Fisher
Photographs show children around the world with their dogs.

Lissy's Friends by Grace Lin
Lissy is lonely on her first day of school, so she makes a bird from origami paper to keep her company. Soon she has a group of folded animal friends. When they blow away, a new friend comes to the rescue.

My Friend Isabelle by Eliza Woloson and Bryan Gough
Isabelle and Charlie are friends who like to be together. It doesn't matter that Charlie is tall and fast, while Isabelle, who has Down's syndrome, is short and takes her time.

We Are Best Friends by Aliki
When a boy's best friend moves away, he learns that he can make new friends and still be loyal to his best one.

When I Was Five by Arthur Howard
A six-year-old boy remembers all the things he loved when he was five. Many of his favorite things have changed, except for his best friend. [featured on a *Between the Lions* episode]

Yo! Yes? by Christopher Raschka
One boy reaches out to another to strike up a new friendship. [featured on a *Between the Lions* episode]

Skill Focus

Concepts of Print (Print Conveys
Meaning, Directionality,
Spaces Between Words)
Writing Names

Theme Connections

Nighttime

Stars

Wish upon a Star

What to Do

- Invite the children to close their eyes and imagine seeing a star in the night sky.
- Ask the children to think of a wish they would like to make. To help the children come up with ideas, ask questions such as, *What do you wish you could play outside? What do you wish we could have for snack?*
- Give each child a large star shape.
- Have the children write or dictate their name on one side of their star.
- Encourage the children to draw a picture of their wish on the other side of their star or to dictate their wishes to you.
- As you write, talk about where you start writing on the paper, the direction in which you write, and the spaces you leave between words. Point to each word as you read the wish to the child.

Cleo and Theo's Book Suggestions

Coyote Places the Stars by Harriet Peck Taylor
A retelling of a Wasco Indian story about how coyote arranges the stars in the shapes of his animal friends.

How the Stars Fell into the Sky: A Navajo Legend
by Jerrie Oughton and Lisa Desmini
This retelling of a Navajo folktale explains the patterns of the stars in the sky.

Star Blanket by Pat Brisson and Erica Magnus
Dad tells his daughter about his favorite childhood blanket. It has 41 stars on it, each representing a relative.

The Star People: A Lakota Story by S. D. Nelson
When a sister and brother are lost in the wilderness, the spirit of their grandmother appears as a star to guide them home.

Vocabulary

ask	question
come true	secret
hope	shape
imagine	sky
names	star
night	wish
outside	

Materials

large cutout star shapes
writing materials

Wondering About Stars

Skill Focus
Concepts of Print (Print Conveys Meaning, Punctuation, Spaces Between Words)
Dictating Sentences

Theme Connections
Nighttime
Stars

Vocabulary

ask
answer
between
letter
question
question mark

spaces
star
twinkle
wonder
word
write

Materials

chart paper
markers
star stickers or drawings

Click on the *Between the Lions* website!
pbskids.org/lions/gryphonhouse

Song: Shower of Stars

Preparation

▣ Write the word *stars* on a large piece of chart paper. Decorate the chart with star stickers or drawings.

What to Do

▣ Ask the children, *What do you know about stars? Do you ever wonder about stars? What would you like to know about stars?*

▣ Read a book about stars (suggestions appear below) and then ask the children to think of a question they have about the stars.

▣ Record each child's questions on the chart next to his or her name. As you write, talk about how you form letters and point out the spaces you leave between words.

▣ Ask, *What do I write at the end of the sentence to show that it is a question? Yes, after each question, I write a question mark.*

▣ Invite each of the children to place a star sticker next to his or her name.

Cleo and Theo's Book Suggestions

I Am a Star by Jean Marzollo and Judith Moffatt
Simple, poetic text and bright cut-paper illustrations explain facts about stars, including why we can't see stars during the day.

Our Stars by Anne Rockwell
A young boy tells us about stars, constellations, planets, and outer space.

Stargazers by Gail Gibbons
This book explains what stars are, how the constellations were named, and more.

Stars by Steve Tomecek
A young boy invites us to learn about the stars and provides answers to common questions.

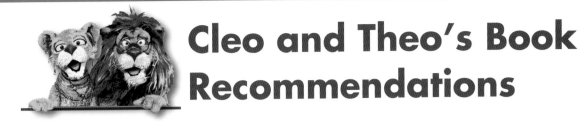

Cleo and Theo's Book Recommendations

Alphabet Books with a Twist

Alphabet Mystery by Audrey Wood
When little x goes missing, the other letters of the alphabet set out to find him. Also see *Alphabet Adventure* by the same author.

The Hidden Alphabet by Laura Vaccaro Seeger
Alphabet letters are hidden in bold graphic images.

K Is for Kiss Good Night by Jill Sardegna
Diverse families tell about their special bedtime routines in this comforting alphabet book. (Look for this out-of-print title in libraries.)

Q Is for Duck: An Alphabet Guessing Game by Michael Folsom
Children learn the sounds that animals make and the sounds that letters make in this clever book of alphabet riddles.

The Turn-Around, Upside-Down Alphabet Book by Lisa Campbell Ernst
In this unusual alphabet book, each letter becomes three different objects when you turn the book in different directions.

Bedtime Stories and Lullabies

All the Pretty Little Horses by Linda Saport
Beautiful pastel illustrations highlight this classic lullaby.

Arrorró, Mi Niño: Latino Lullabies and Gentle Games by Lulu Delacre
A collection of lullabies and finger plays from various Latin American countries.

Bedtime for Little Bears! by David Bedford
When a polar bear cub refuses to go to sleep, his mother takes him for a walk so he can see how other animals prepare for bed.

Close Your Eyes by Kate Banks
A tiger cub refuses to nap, insisting he'll miss seeing his favorite things.

Hush, Little Baby by Brian Pinkney
In this version of the classic lullaby, Dad does what he can to soothe his young daughter while Mama does errands.

Sleep, Black Bear, Sleep by Jane Yolen
Rhyming text tells how a variety of animals settle down for their winter naps.

Sleepy Bears by Mem Fox
Six cubs refuse to settle down until their mother recites a unique rhyming tale that soothes each one.

Time to Sleep by Denise Fleming
Changes in the weather let bear know that it's time for his winter rest. He lets other animals know that it is time to start hibernating.

Where Is Bear? by Leslea Newman
In this rhyming tale, forest animals play hide-and-seek, but Bear can't be found. Where can he be? See also *Skunk's Spring Surprise* by the same author.

Books About Birthdays

Alicia's Happy Day by Meg Starr
In this bilingual book, everyone greets Alicia as she walks home with her loving extended family.

A Birthday for Cow! by Jan Thomas
Pig and Mouse are going to make Cow "the best birthday cake EVER!" and they aren't too keen about Duck's idea to add a turnip. [featured on a *Between the Lions* episode]

Birthday Presents by Cynthia Rylant
On the eve of her sixth birthday, a girl and her parents reminisce about birthday celebrations.

Birthdays! Celebrating Life Around the World by Eve B. Feldman
Simple text and paintings by children show how birthdays are celebrated around the world.

Happy Birthday, Jamela! by Niki Daly
A young South African girl has to get plain shoes for her birthday outfit. When she makes her shoes more festive, a local artist notices.

Henry's First-Moon Birthday by Lenore Look
A young girl helps her grandmother prepare a traditional Chinese celebration to welcome the arrival of her baby brother.

Jamaica Louise James by Amy Hest
On her eighth birthday, a girl receives paints that she uses to brighten the subway station where Grammy works. [featured on a *Between the Lions* episode]

Miss Spider's ABC by David Kirk
In this alphabet book, Miss Spider's insect friends gather for her surprise birthday party.

Uno, Dos, Tres: One, Two, Three by Pat Mora
In this rhythmic counting book, two sisters have fun in a Mexican market choosing presents for their mother's birthday.

The Secret Birthday Message by Eric Carle
Tim gets a secret, coded message for his birthday. Children can join in as he looks through the clues to find his birthday surprise.

Books About Clothing

All Kinds of Clothes by Jeri S. Cipriano
This nonfiction book describes the clothing people wear to keep themselves warm or cool.

Bear Gets Dressed: A Guessing Game Story by Harriet Ziefert
The reader looks at pictures of clothes to guess what Bear will wear in different kinds of weather.

Charlie Needs a Cloak by Tomie dePaola
A shepherd shears his sheep, cards and spins the wool, weaves and dyes the cloth, and sews a lovely new red cloak.

The Emperor's New Clothes by Hans Christian Andersen
An emperor gets tricked into wearing an invisible suit of clothes.

Hats, Hats, Hats by Ann Morris
Learn about the many different hats worn around the world.

Jamaica and Brianna by Juanita Havill
Jamaica hates wearing her hand-me-down boots, especially when her friend, Brianna, has pink fuzzy ones.

Jesse Bear, What Will You Wear? by Nancy White Carlstrom
Find out what Jesse Bear wears while he romps through a bright and sunny day.

Joseph Had a Little Overcoat by Simms Taback
A very old overcoat is recycled numerous times into a variety of garments. [featured on a *Between the Lions* episode]

Mary Wore Her Red Dress and Henry Wore His Green Sneakers by Merle Peek
Each of Katy Bear's animal friends attends her birthday party wearing different colors of clothing.

Miss Mary Mack: A Hand-Clapping Rhyme adapted by Mary Ann Hoberman
A hand-clapping rhyme about a girl dressed in black, with music and directions for clapping.

Mud Puddle by Robert N. Munsch
Every time Julie Ann goes outside, a mud puddle jumps up and dirties her clothes—but soap saves the day.

New Clothes for New Year's Day by Hyun-joo Bae
Follow the adventures of a young Korean girl as she prepares for the Lunar New Year.

A New Coat for Anna by Harriet Ziefert
Anna's mother trades the few possessions she has left to get a new coat for Anna.

New Shoes for Sylvia by Johanna Hurwitz
Sylvia gets a pair of beautiful red shoes from her Tia Rosita and finds ways to use them until she grows big enough for them to fit.

A Rainbow All Around Me by Sandra Pinkney
A multi-ethnic cast of children dress in each color of the rainbow.

Red Parka Mary by Peter Eyvindson
For Christmas, a boy gives his elderly neighbor a red parka to keep her warm. [featured on a *Between the Lions* episode]

Suki's Kimono by Chieri Uegaki
Instead of wearing something new on her first day of school, Suki wears the blue cotton kimono that her grandmother gave her last summer.

The Tale of Benjamin Bunny by Beatrix Potter
Benjamin Bunny convinces Peter to return to Mr. McGregor's garden for his lost clothing.

Two Pair of Shoes by Esther Sanderson
Maggie, a young Cree girl, receives two pairs of shoes for her birthday: black, patent leather shoes and handmade beaded moccasins.

To help children enjoy and love books, read aloud to them at least three times a day.

Books About Colors, Art, Art Appreciation

Fiction and Poetry

Bottle Houses: The Creative World of Grandma Prisbey by Melissa Eskridge Slaymaker
This picture book biography tells the story of a woman who used glass bottles and other junk-yard finds to build a unique, colorful home.

Cherries and Cherry Pits by Vera B. Williams
Whenever Bidemmi draws, she tells the story of what she is drawing.

Color Farm by Lois Elhert
The author/artist combines colorful cut-out shapes to make pictures of farm animals.

The Colors of Us by Karen Katz
A young girl mixes colors to paint pictures of her family and friends in all their different shades.

Cows Can't Fly by David Milgrim
In this rhyming tale, a herd of cows take flight after seeing a boy's fanciful drawing.

The Dot by Peter H. Reynolds
Vashti thinks she can't draw, but her teacher suggests "Just make a mark and see where it takes you." (Also see *Ish* by the same author.)

Dream Carver by Diana Cohn
A boy is inspired by his dreams and imagination to create life-size, colorful animals carved out of wood. [featured on a *Between the Lions* episode]

Harold and the Purple Crayon by Crockett Johnson
This classic tale about a young boy and his crayon celebrates the imagination.

Jamaica Louise James by Amy Hest
For a birthday surprise, eight-year-old Jamaica and her mom decorate the subway station where her grandmother works. (Also see *Nana's Birthday Party* by the same author.) [*Jamaica Louise James* by Amy Hest featured on a *Between the Lions* episode]

Let's Make Rabbits by Leo Lionni
A pencil and a pair of scissors each make a rabbit and the rabbits become best friends.

Lily Brown's Paintings by Angela Johnson
Lily loves her family and the world around her. Using her imagination, she captures her joy in a series of whimsical paintings.

The Lion and the Little Red Bird by Elisa Kleven
A little bird is delighted to discover an artistic lion who uses his tail as a brush to create colorful paintings.

My Colors, My World/Mis Colores, Mi Mundo by Maya Christina Gonzalez
A girl living in the desert describes the colors that remind her of the people and places she loves.

Pablo the Artist by Satoshi Kitamura
An unusual dream gives Pablo a brilliant idea of what to paint for an upcoming art exhibition. [featured on a *Between the Lions* episode]

Patches Lost and Found by Steven Kroll
Jenny, a reluctant writer but prolific artist, draws and then writes a story about losing, then finding, her pet guinea pig.

Red Is a Dragon by Roseanne Thong
The colors that surround a young Chinese-American girl remind her of the things that she loves.

Spicy Hot Colors: Colores Picantes by Sherry Shahan
Colors explode off the page in this energetic, jazzy picture book introducing readers to colors in English and Spanish. [featured on a *Between the Lions* episode]

The Tale of Pip and Squeak by Kate Duke
Pip doesn't like the sound of his brother's singing, and Squeak doesn't like the smell of his brother's paints, but they work together to solve an emergency.

Yellow Elephant: A Bright Bestiary by Julie Larios
Rhyming poems describe a variety of colorful animals.

Nonfiction Book
Elephants Can Paint Too! by Katya Arnold
This true story is written by an artist who taught kids and elephants in Thailand how to paint. [featured on a *Between the Lions* episode]

To help children enjoy and love books, read aloud to them at least three times a day.

Books About Families

Fiction and Poetry

Abuela by Arthur Dorros
A girl and her grandmother go on an adventure, flying above the streets of New York City.

Bigmama's by Donald Crews
The author fondly remembers family visits to his grandmother's farm when he was a small boy.

Brave Georgie Goat by Denis Roche
In three stories, Georgie Goat overcomes her anxieties, including her fear that her mommy won't come back at the end of the day.

Buzz by Janet Wong
An Asian-American child watches as his mommy and daddy get ready for work.

Corduroy by Don Freeman
A stuffed bear waits hopefully in a department store until he finds a home with a little girl who hugs and loves him. Also by the same author: *A Pocket for Corduroy*.

Count the Ways, Little Brown Bear by Jonathan London
Mama Brown Bear assures her cub how much she loves him in this bedtime counting book.

Do Like Kyla by Angela Johnson
On a snowy day, a young girl imitates her big sister from morning to night. Also by the same author: *Daddy Calls Me Man, When I Am Old with You.*

Grandfather and I by Helen Buckley
A child tenderly relates how Grandfather is the perfect person to spend time with because he is never in a hurry. Also by the same author: *Grandmother and I.*

The Happy Hocky Family Moves to the Country! by Lane Smith
The adventures of the Hocky family continue after they move from the city to the country. [featured on a *Between the Lions* episode]

I Love You Because You're You by Liz Baker
In rhyme, a mother describes her love for her child no matter what he does.

I Love You Like Crazy Cakes by Rose Lewis
A mother describes going to China to adopt a baby girl.

Jamaica's Find by Juanita Havill
When Jamaica brings a stuffed animal that she finds in the park to the lost-and-found, she makes a new friend.

Kevin and His Dad by Irene Smalls
Kevin has a great time spending a day doing chores and playing with his dad. Also by the same author: *My Nana and Me, My Pop Pop and Me.*

Mama, Do You Love Me? By Barbara Joosse
A child living in the Artic learns that a mother's love is unconditional.

Mama Zooms by Jane Cowen-Fletcher
Mama has a zooming machine—a wheelchair that she uses to zoom everywhere.

Missing: One Stuffed Rabbit by Maryann Cocca-Leffler
When Josie takes the class pet, Coco the stuffed rabbit, home for the weekend, she loses him in the mall.

A Mother for Choco by Keiko Kasza
A lonely bird named Choco finds a mother who holds him, kisses him, and cheers him up.

My Dog Is as Smelly as Dirty Socks by Hanoch Piven
A little girl describes her family members through humorous portraits she's made of them using everyday objects. [featured on a *Between the Lions* episode]

Night on Neighborhood Street by Eloise Greenfield
Poems paint a vivid portrait of urban life.

Oh My Baby, Little One by Kathi Appelt
A soothing, lyrical story about the ways Baby Bird can keep Mama Bird's love with him, even when she's far away.

Olivia and the Missing Toy by Ian Falkoner
While Olivia helps her mother make a soccer uniform, her stuffed toy goes missing.

Owl Moon by Jane Yolen
A father and daughter share a special family tradition when they trek through the snowy woods at night to find a great horned owl.

Quinito's Neighborhood by Ina Cumpiano
A young boy takes readers on a tour of his neighborhood and the people who live there. (bilingual English/Spanish text)

The Very Best Daddy of All by Marion Dane Bauer
Pictures and rhyming text show how some fathers—animal, bird, and human—take care of their children.

Waddle, Waddle, Quack, Quack, Quack by Barbara Anne Skalak
While out exploring, a duckling is separated from his mama and the rest of the family.

With My Brother/Con mi hermano by Eileen Moe
A young boy enjoys spending time with his brother and hopes to be like him when he gets older. (bilingual English/Spanish text)

Nonfiction

Animal Babies by Harry Mcnaught
Simple text and color illustrations describe baby animals and their mothers.

Baby Owls by Aubrey Lang
Photographs and words tell the life cycle of baby great horned owls.

Be My Neighbor by Maya Ajmera and John Ivanko
Photos show neighborhoods around the world where children live, play, worship, and work.

Families by Ann Morris
This photo essay shows that children all around the world are part of families—big and small, loving, sharing, and caring for one another.

Families Are Different by Nina Pellegrini
Korean girl, adopted by an American family, looks at different types of families.

Lots of Moms by Shelly Rotner
This photo essay shows lots of moms and their children working, helping, and playing together. Also by the same author: *Lots of Dads.*

Owls by Adrienne Mason
Kids can find out where owls live, what they eat, how young owls learn, and more.

You and Me Together: Moms, Dads, and Kids Around the World by Barbara Kerley
Beautiful photographs show parents and children around the world as they laugh, work, play and eat together.

Books About Feelings

Alexander and the Terrible, Horrible, No Good, Very Bad Day by Judith Viorst
Alexander has such a bad day that he vows to move to Australia.

Feelings by Shelley Rotner
Color photographs of children and simple text introduce a range of emotions.

The Grouchy Ladybug by Eric Carle
An ill-tempered ladybug goes through the day picking fights with various animals until she realizes that it is better to be pleasant.

The Hello, Goodbye Window by Norton Juster
While visiting her grandparents, a young girl feels happy and sad when she sees her parents coming to pick her up.

If You're Happy and You Know It by Jane Cabrera
Animals sing different verses of the popular song.

The Leaving Morning by Angela Johnson
A brother and sister say goodbye to familiar people and places before they move.

Sam Is Never Scared by Thierry Robberecht
Sam acts as though he isn't scared of anything, though at night he secretly worries that monsters are hiding in his room.

Sometimes I'm Bombaloo by Rachel Vail
Katie is a nice girl, but when her baby brother knocks over the castle she's building, she gets mad . . . so mad that she's Bombaloo!

Today I Feel Silly & Other Moods That Make My Day by Jamie Lee Curtis
Young readers identify and explore their many emotions as they read about a young girl whose mood changes from silly to angry to excited.

Walter Was Worried by Laura Vaccaro Seeger
This alphabet book explores children's emotional reactions to a storm.

When Sophie Gets Angry—Really, Really Angry by Molly Bang
Sophie becomes furious when her mother tells her it's her sister's turn to play with her favorite stuffed gorilla. After some time away, Sophie is able to calm herself down.

When You Are Happy by Eileen Spinelli
A girl is reassured that no matter how she may feel when she is sick, lost, or lonely, her family is there to comfort her and make her feel better.

Why Do You Cry?: Not a Sob Story by Kate Klise
Little Rabbit discovers that everyone cries sometimes.

Yesterday I Had the Blues by Jeron Ashford Frame
A young boy uses colors to capture a range of emotions, from "down in my shoes blues" to the kind of greens that "make you want to be Somebody." [featured on a *Between the Lions* episode]

To help children enjoy and love books, read aloud to them at least three times a day.

Books About Food

Fiction

A Birthday for Cow! by Jan Thomas
Pig and Mouse are going to make Cow "the best birthday cake EVER!" and they aren't too keen about Duck's idea to add a turnip. [featured on a *Between the Lions* episode]

Bee-bim Bop! by Linda Sue Park
In playful verse with a bouncy beat a young girl describes how her mom makes the popular Korean dish called Bee-bim bop. [featured on a *Between the Lions* episode]

Bread Is for Eating by David and Phillis Gershator
A mother sings a song to help her son appreciate the bread that he leaves on his plate. Bilingual text.

Chicks & Salsa by Aaron Reynolds
The chickens at Nuthatcher Farm get tired of the same old food, so the rooster cooks up a plan for a tasty fiesta. [featured on a *Between the Lions* episode]

Dim Sum for Everyone! by Grace Lin
While eating dim sum at a Chinese restaurant, family members choose a favorite item from carts brought to their table.

Dumpling Soup by Jama Kim Rattigan
A Hawaiian family gathers at grandma's house to make dumplings for a New Year's celebration.

Everybody Cooks Rice by Norah Dooley
A young girl discovers that all of her neighbors, despite their different backgrounds, eat rice. (See also *Everybody Brings Noodles* and *Everybody Bakes Bread* by the same author.)

Jalapeño Bagels by Natasha Wing
It's International Day at school and Pablo, whose father is Jewish and whose mother is Mexican, must decide what to bring. Includes recipes.

Let's Eat by Ana Zamorano
Every day Antonio's mother tries to get everyone to sit down together to eat, but someone is always busy elsewhere.

Little Pea by Amy Krouse Rosenthal
Little Pea's parents insist that he finish eating all of his candy before he can have dessert—a big bowl of spinach!

Mama Provi and the Pot of Rice by Sylvia Rosa-Casanova
Mama Provi makes *arroz con pollo* for her granddaughter, who has the chicken pox.

Market Day by Lois Ehlert
Rhyming text and art objects tell of a family's day at a farmer's market.

Stone Soup by Heather Forest
Two hungry and clever travelers teach a town a lesson in sharing. Includes a soup recipe.

Tortillas and Lullabies/Tortillas y cancioncitas by Lynn Reiser
Large colorful paintings show three generations sharing family traditions, including making tortillas.

Yum Yum Dim Sum by Amy Wilson Sanger
Collage illustrations and simple text introduces dim sum to children. See also *First Book of Sushi,¡Hola! Jalapeño, A Little Bit of Soul Food, Let's Nosh!,* and *Mangia! Mangia!* by the same author.

Nonfiction

Bread Bread Bread by Ann Morris and Ken Heyman
Simple text and color photos describe and show the different kinds of bread that people eat around the world.

Where Does Food Come From? by Shelley Rotner and Gary Goss
Photographs and text show the natural source of many of the foods children enjoy.

Books About Friends

Aggie and Ben: Three Stories by Lori Ries
In this trio of simple stories, Ben gets a dog that instantly becomes his best friend.

Be Quiet, Marina! by Kirsten DeBear
Simple text and photographs tell about the friendship between Marina, a noisy girl with cerebral palsy, and Moira, a quiet girl with Down's syndrome.

Bein' with You This Way by W. Nikola-Lisa
A group of children playing together in the park celebrate their differences. [adapted for a *Between the Lions* episode]

Being Friends by Karen Beaumont
Despite their differences, two girls know that the key to friendship is having one special thing in common: they like being friends.

Best Best Friends by Margaret Chodos-Irvine
Mary and Clare are best friends, but when Mary gets special attention on her birthday, a jealous Clare is mean to her friend. After a while, they find a way to be friends again.

Earl's Too Cool for Me by Leah Komaiko and Laura Cornell
Even though Earl is so cool that he "taught an octopus how to scrub," he's willing to make new friends. [featured on a *Between the Lions* episode]

Friends at School by Rochelle Bunnett
Photographs and text tell the story of a diverse group of children, some with disabilities, who are friends at school.

How to Lose All Your Friends by Nancy Carlson
This book tells what to do to make sure that you don't have any friends. In the process, children learn positive behaviors that help them make and get along with friends.

Jamaica's Find by Juanita Havill
Jamaica makes a new friend at the park when she returns a stuffed animal to the Lost and Found. See also *Jamaica and Brianna* by the same author.

A Kid's Best Friend by Maya Ajmera and Alex Fisher
Photographs show children around the world with their dogs.

Knuffle Bunny Too: A Case of Mistaken Identity by Mo Willems
Trixie is excited to bring Knuffle Bunny to her first day at preschool, until she sees Sonja with a Knuffle Bunny of her own. After a bunny mix-up, the girls become friends.

Lissy's Friends by Grace Lin
Lissy is lonely on her first day of school, so she makes a bird from origami paper to keep her company. Soon she has a group of folded animal friends. When they blow away, a new friend comes to the rescue.

Little Blue and Little Yellow by Leo Lionni
A blue dot and a yellow dot are best friends. One day when they hug, they become a green dot.

Matthew and Tilly by Rebecca C. Jones
After best friends Matthew and Tilly argue over a broken crayon, they apologize and find a way to be friends again.

My Friend and I by Lisa Jahn-Clough
A girl and a boy fight over a stuffed bunny and rip its ear. They separate in anger. Soon, the girl apologizes and finds a way to fix the bunny.

My Friend Isabelle by Eliza Woloson
Isabelle and Charlie are friends who like to be together. It doesn't matter that Charlie is tall and fast, while Isabelle, who has Down's syndrome, is short and takes her time.

Sand Castle by Brenda Shannon Yee
Jen is building a sand castle at the beach. One-by-one, new friends join her, each adding a new element to the structure.

Simon and Molly Plus Hester by Lisa Jahn-Clough
Simon and Molly play together every day, but when Hester joins them, Simon worries that Molly doesn't like him anymore.

This Is Our House by Michael Rosen
George won't let the other children play in his cardboard box house. When he leaves, the kids take over and teach George that there is room for everyone.

We Are Best Friends by Aliki
When a boy's best friend moves away, he learns that he can make new friends and still be loyal to his best one.

When I Was Five by Arthur Howard
A six-year-old boy remembers all the things he loved when he was five. Many of his favorite things have changed, except for his best friend. [featured on a *Between the Lions* episode]

Will I Have a Friend? by Miriam Cohen
Jim is nervous on his first day of school. He doesn't know anyone, and doesn't know if he will find anyone to be his friend.

Yo! Yes? by Christopher Raschka
One boy reaches out to another to strike up a new friendship. [featured on a *Between the Lions* episode]

> **To help children enjoy and love books, read aloud to them at least three times a day.**

Books About Helping

Big Dog . . . Little Dog: A Bedtime Story by P.D. Eastman
This story about two dogs illustrates the concepts of size, color, and opposites.

Borreguita and the Coyote by Verna Aardema
A little lamb outwits a fierce coyote in this colorful retelling of a Mexican folktale.

Cucumber Soup by Vickie Leigh Krudwig
Ten black ants and a tiny flea move a cucumber.

The Enormous Turnip by Aleksei Tolstoy (illustrated by Scott Goto)
This is a retelling of the classic tale for young readers.

Fables from Aesop adapted and illustrated by Tom Lynch
"The Lion and the Mouse" is included in this collection of Aesop's fables.

The Giant Cabbage: An Alaska Folktale by Chérie B. Stihler
Set in Alaska, this retelling features native wildlife.

The Giant Carrot by Jan Peck
The Russian folktale is retold as a Texas yarn.

The Gigantic Turnip by Aleksei Tolstoy (illustrated by Niamh Sharkey)
Only when a tiny mouse joins in can a group uproot this giant vegetable.

Grandma Lena's Big Ol' Turnip by Denia Lewis Hester
This retelling of *The Gigantic Turnip* is about teamwork, sharing, and cooking in an extended African-American family.

How the Chipmunk Got His Stripes by Joseph and James Bruchac
In this Native American tale, a little squirrel challenges a big bear and is transformed into a chipmunk.

Just What Mama Needs by Sharlee Mullins Glenn and Amiko Hirao
Abby loves dressing up in different costumes, and her mom enjoys finding ways a pirate, a detective, and a genie can help with chores around the house each day of the week. [featured on a *Between the Lions* episode]

The Lion and the Mouse by Carol Jones
In this adaptation, an adventurous mouse leaves his home on a ship and saves the king of the jungle.

Mole and the Baby Bird by Marjorie Newman
Mole discovers the best way to help a baby bird that has fallen out of its nest. [featured on a *Between the Lions* episode]

Red Parka Mary by Peter Eyvindson
In this heartwarming story, a boy overcomes his fears to help an elderly neighbor, and she gives him "the biggest gift in the whole wide world." [featured on a *Between the Lions* episode]

Watch Out! Big Bro's Coming by Jez Alborough
The animals tremble at the news about "big bro," until it turns out to be tiny mouse's older brother.

Books About Libraries

Fiction

ABC Letters in the Library by Bonnie Farmer
An alliterative ABC book about what is in the library.

Armando Asked, "Why?" by Jay Hulbert and Sid Kantor
With his family's help, inquisitive Armando discovers that the library has books that can answer his questions.

Beatrice Doesn't Want To by Laura Numeroff
When her older brother takes her to the library, Beatrice discovers the wonders of books.

Book! Book! Book! by Deborah Bruss
When the children go back to school, the animals on the farm are bored, so they go visit the library.

D.W.'s Library Card by Marc Brown
D.W. is eager to get a library card so she can take out any book she wants.

I.Q. Goes to the Library by Mary Ann Fraser
I.Q., the class pet, goes to the library with his class and learns all about books and libraries.

Molly at the Library by Ruth Radlauer
Four-year-old Molly goes to the library with her father and is thrilled to discover she can take home 10 books.

Once Inside the Library by Barbara A. Huff
This simple story tells about the different adventures that books can bring.

Red Light, Green Light, Mama and Me by Cari Best
Lizzie spends the day in the city at the public library helping her mother, a children's librarian.

Nonfiction

Check It Out! The Book About Libraries by Gail Gibbons
This book describes libraries and how they work.

I Like the Library by Anne Rockwell
Simple text tells about the materials you can find and take home from the library.

Tomás and the Library Lady by Pat Mora
This biography tells the true story of how a librarian helped open the world of books to the son of migrant farm workers.

Books About Music

Fiction

Charlie Parker Played Be Bop by Chris Raschka
Shoes, birds, lollipops, and letters dance across the pages to the beat of Charlie Parker's saxophone music. [featured on a *Between the Lions* episode]

Ms. McDonald Has a Class by Jan Ormerod
This variation of the "Old MacDonald" song tells about a kindergarten class that visits a farm.

Music Is by Lloyd Moss
A rhyming tribute to the many ways people enjoy music.

Music, Music for Everyone by Vera B. Williams
Rosa plays her accordion with her friends in the Oak Street Band and earns money to help her sick grandmother.

Ruby Sings the Blues by Niki Daly
Ruby's voice is SO loud, it's driving everyone crazy, until her jazz-playing neighbors come up with a plan and Ruby learns to sing without everyone needing earplugs. [featured on a *Between the Lions* episode]

Violet's Music by Angela Johnson
Violet plays music every chance she gets, and she's always looking for other kids who think and dream music all day long. [featured on a *Between the Lions* episode]

Nonfiction and Concept Books

Ah, Music! by Aliki
A beginner's guide to composers, instruments, artists, and performers, this book includes facts about music history and genres.

The Jazzy Alphabet by Sherry Shahan and Mary Thelan
The letters in this alphabet book boogie.

M Is for Music by Kathleen Krull
This alphabet book introduces musical terms, from anthem to zydeco.

My Family Plays Music by Judy Cox
Each member of a girl's family plays a different instrument and enjoys a different type of music—from bluegrass to hymns.

Sing-Along Books

Arroz con leche: Popular Songs and Rhymes from Latin America by Lulu Delacre
This book offers a sample of popular children's songs throughout Latin America. In English and Spanish. (book and audiotape)

Baby Beluga by Raffi
Illustrations accompany the lyrics to this popular song about a little white whale.

Catalina Magdalena Hoopensteiner Wallendiner Hogan Logan Bogan Was Her Name by Tedd Arnold
The author transforms a traditional camp song into a wild, wacky book about a deliriously happy young girl with an unusually long name.

Shake It to the One That You Love the Best by Cheryl Warren Mattox, Varnette P. Honeywood, and Brenda Joysmith
This is an illustrated collection of 26 play songs from the African American musical tradition. (book and audiotape)

> **To help children enjoy and love books, read aloud to them at least three times a day.**

Books About Nighttime and Bedtime

Bear Snores On by Karma Wilson
  A hibernating bear wakes up to find his cave full of uninvited guests having a party without him. [featured on a *Between the Lions* episode]

Daytime and Nighttime Animals by Barbara Behm and Mark Carwardine
  Animals are categorized based on the time of day they are active.

Fiona Loves the Night by Patricia MacLachlan and Emily MacLachlan Charest
  A young girl wakes and experiences the mysterious beauty of the night.

Goodnight Moon by Margaret Wise Brown
  In this classic bedtime story, a young rabbit says goodnight to each of the objects in his room.

Grandfather Twilight by Barbara Helen Berger
  Grandfather Twilight goes for a walk through the woods as the day draws to a close.

Here Comes the Night by Anne Rockwell
  In this soothing story, a mother and son go through their nighttime ritual.

Kitten's First Full Moon by Kevin Henkes
  A young kitten sets out in search of the bowl of milk she sees in the sky. After a night of adventure she returns home, which is the best place to be.

Little Night by Yuyi Morales
  As the day comes to an end, Mother Sky fills a bathtub with stars and calls to Little Night. But Little Night still wants to play!

Long Night Moon by Cynthia Rylant
  Twelve magical poems and beautiful illustrations trace the moon through the cycle of the year.

The Night Eater by Ana Juan
  Every morning the Night Eater gobbles up all the darkness of night. But what happens when the Night Eater doesn't come?

Night in the Country by Cynthia Rylant
  Lyrical text and rich, color-pencil drawings shine a light on the activities and sounds that happen in the dark. [featured on a *Between the Lions* episode]

Night Shift Daddy by Eileen Spinelli
  A girl shares a nighttime ritual with her father who works the night shift. Roles are reversed, and the ritual is repeated when dad comes home.

The Night Worker by Kate Banks
  A boy goes to work with his father, a construction engineer who works at night.

One Nighttime Sea by Deborah Lee Rose
  Count nighttime animals that live in the sea in this rhythmic counting book.

Owl Moon by Jane Yolen
  A girl and her father set out on a cold winter night to find a great-horned owl.

The Owl Who Was Afraid of the Dark by Jill Tomlinson
  An owlet who is afraid of the dark asks animals and people why they like the dark. Their answers convince him that nighttime is not so scary.

Sleepy Little Owl by Howard Goldsmith
  A baby owl plays with his daytime friends, but as he fights to stay awake, he learns that he truly is a night owl.

Snuggle Up, Sleepy Ones by Claire Freedman
  As night descends on the jungle, young animals snuggle up to their parents.

So Sleepy Story by Uri Shulevitz
  A boy is sound asleep until music drifts through his window, causing the boy and everything in his house to dance.

A South African Night by Rachel Isadora
  Contrasts the activities of people in a city during the day to the activities of the animals at night in a South African nature preserve.

Sweet Dreams: How Animals Sleep by Kimiko Kajikawa
  Photos and rhyming text showcase animals at rest.

When I'm Sleepy by Jane R. Howard
  As a girl goes to bed, she wonders what it would be like to sleep as the animals do.

When Sheep Sleep by Laura Numeroff
  When the sheep she is counting fall asleep, a wide-awake girl tries to count other animals, only to discover that they are sleeping too!

Books About Seasons

Animals in Winter by Henrietta Bancroft
  Simple, factual text and illustrations show what animals do in the winter.

Autumn: An Alphabet Acrostic by Stephen Schnur
  A fall-related riddle is presented for each letter of the alphabet.

Bear Wants More by Karma Wilson
  In this sequel to *Bear Snores On*, it's spring and Bear is hungry after his long winter sleep. No matter how much he eats, Bear still wants more. For more stories about Bear, see *Bear Gets Sick* and *Bear's New Friend* by the same author.

Come On, Rain! by Karen Hesse
  In the middle of the summer heat, a girl gathers her friends to wait for the long-awaited rain.

Hurray For Spring! by Patricia Hubbell
  A boy celebrates spring's arrival by doing a variety of activities.

It's Fall by Linda Glaser
  A boy explores the changes that happen in the fall. See also *It's Spring, It's Summer*, and *It's Winter* by the same author.

A Kitten Tale by Eric Rohmann
  Three kittens grow anxious as the seasons pass and winter draws near.

Listen, Listen by Phillis Gershator
  An ode to the sights and sounds of the changing seasons.

Summer Sun Risin' by W. Nikola-Lisa
  A boy marks the passage of the sun as he spends the day on the family farm.

Thirteen Moons on Turtle's Back: A Native American Year of Moons by Joseph Bruchac and Jonathan London
  Native American poems celebrate the passing of a year.

Wake Up, It's Spring! by Lisa Campbell Ernst
  As the sun warms the earth, one-by-one animals wake and celebrate spring.

What Is Hibernation? by John Crossingham and Bobbie Kalman
  Photographs and text show animals hibernating and explain why it happens.

Winter Is the Warmest Season by Lauren Stringer
  For the boy in this story, hot chocolate, fuzzy boots, and hissing radiators make winter the warmest season. [featured on a *Between the Lions* episode]

Winter Lullaby by Barbara Seuling
  This rhyming concept book shows what various animals do during the winter.

Books About Sounds and Listening

City Lullaby by Marilyn Singer
   Lively poems transform the sounds of the city into a lullaby for a sleepy baby.

Good-Night, Owl! by Pat Hutchins
   An owl tries to sleep during the day but is constantly awakened by the sounds of other animals.

The Listening Walk by Paul Showers
   A girl and her father take a special walk and listen to the sounds around them.

Night in the Country by Cynthia Rylant
   Lyrical text and rich, color-pencil drawings shine a light on the activities and sounds that happen in the dark. [featured on a *Between the Lions* episode]

Sounds All Around by Wendy Pfeffer
   This book in the Let's-Read-and-Find-Out Science series offers a simple explanation of sounds and hearing, including how animals hear.

Sounds of the Wild: Nighttime by Maurice Pledger
   This nonfiction book describes sounds made by night animals in different parts of the world.

Books About Stars

Fiction

Coyote Places the Stars by Harriet Peck Taylor
   A retelling of a Wasco Indian story about how coyote arranges the stars in the shapes of his animal friends.

Draw Me a Star by Eric Carle
   An artist's drawing of a star sparks the creation of an entire universe.

How the Stars Fell into the Sky: A Navajo Legend by Jerrie Oughton
   This retelling of a Navajo folktale explains the patterns of the stars in the sky.

How to Catch a Star by Oliver Jeffers
   A young stargazer decides he would like to catch a star. Although his attempts fail, he finds a starfish on the beach that makes him happy.

SkySisters by Jan Bourdeau Waboose
   Two Ojibway sisters silently watch the midnight dance of the SkySpirits—the Northern Lights.

Star Blanket by Pat Brisson
   Dad tells his daughter about his favorite childhood blanket. It has forty-one stars on it, each representing a relative.

The Star People: A Lakota Story by S.D. Nelson
   When a sister and brother are lost in the wilderness, the spirit of their grandmother appears as a star to guide them home.

Stella the Star by Mark Shulman
   Stella tells her parents that she will be the star in the school play. The surprise ending plays on the double meaning of the word *star*.

There Was a Bold Lady Who Wanted a Star by Charise Mericle Harper
   In this variation on the traditional cumulative rhyme, a feisty woman tries roller skates, a bicycle, and even a rocket to reach a star!

To help children enjoy and love books, read aloud to them at least three times a day.

Nonfiction and Concept Books

The Big Dipper by Franklyn M. Branley
This book in the Let's-Read-and-Find-Out Science series explains basic facts about the Big Dipper.

I Am a Star by Jean Marzollo
Simple, poetic text and bright cut-paper illustrations explain facts about stars, including why we can't see stars during the day.

Once Upon a Starry Night: A Book of Constellations by Jacqueline Mitton
This book presents ten constellations and retells the Greek myths related to them. Includes information about the solar system.

Our Solar System by Seymour Simon
This book for older readers features color photographs of the sun, planets, moons, asteroids, meteoroids, and comets.

Our Stars by Anne Rockwell
A young boy tells us about stars, constellations, planets, and outer space.

Postcards from Pluto: A Tour of the Solar System by Loreen Leedy
A group of children take a tour of the solar system and send home postcards describing the planets.

Stargazers by Gail Gibbons
This book explains what stars are, how the constellations were named, and more.

Stars by Seymour Simon
This book for older readers discusses the composition and characteristics of stars, with color photographs.

Stars by Steve Tomecek
A young boy invites us to learn about the stars and provides answers to common questions.

Zoo in the Sky: A Book of Animal Constellations by Jacqueline Mitton
This book introduces children to the constellations that are named for animals—Leo the Lion, Great Bear and Little Bear, and more. Includes star maps that show the constellations.

Poems and Songs

The Earth Under Sky Bear's Feet: Native American Poems of the Land by Joseph Bruchac
A collection of 12 story poems about the night sky from various North American Indian cultures.

I Like Stars by Margaret Wise Brown
A simple poem describes all kinds of stars that appear in the night sky.

The Sun, the Moon, and the Stars by Nancy Elizabeth Wallace
A collection of 33 poems about the sun, the moon, and the stars, illustrated with cut-paper art.

Twinkle, Twinkle, Little Star by Sylvia Long
Watercolor pictures of young animals gazing at the stars and returning home to their parents illustrate the verses of the traditional lullaby.

Books About the Concepts of Big and Little

Big and Little by Margaret Miller
Photos of adults and children of varying ages demonstrate the concepts of big and little.

Big and Little by Samantha Berger
Labeled photographs compare large and small dogs, houses, hands, and more.

Big and Little by Steve Jenkins
This book illustrates the concept of size by comparing different animals.

My Very First Look at Sizes by Christiane Gunzi
This board book uses colorful photographs of various objects to introduce the concept of size.

Size: A First Poem Book About Size by Felicia Law
Ten simple poems illustrate the concept of size.

Books Illustrated by G. Brian Karas

The Class Artist by G. Brian Karas
Fred is excited about the class art assignment but experiences "artist's block."

How Many Seeds in a Pumpkin by Margaret McNamara
A class tries to guess how many seeds are in a large, medium, and small pumpkin.

Muncha! Muncha! Muncha! by Candace Fleming
A farmer tries to keep his greens safe from a trio of hungry bunnies.

On Earth by G. Brian Karas
This concept book explains the earth and its cycles, including the seasons.

The Seals on the Bus by Lenny Hort
Animals take a wild ride in this variation of "The Wheels on the Bus."

Books Written and Illustrated by Cathryn Falwell

Butterflies for Kiri
A package of origami paper helps a young girl learn that an artist can use her materials in different ways.

Feast for 10
In this lively counting book, a large family prepares for dinner.

Shape Space
In simple rhyming text, a girl explores basic shapes as she dances.

We Have a Baby
A family prepares for the arrival of the new baby.

To help children enjoy and love books, read aloud to them at least three times a day.

Cookbooks

Children's Quick and Easy Cookbook by Angela Wilkes
Full-color photographs show how to make each recipe.

Cook and Learn: Recipes, Songs, and Activities for Children by Adrienne Wiland
Simple, no-bake recipes are accompanied by music, art, and other activities for families.

I'm the Chef: The Young Chef's Mexican Cookbook by Crabtree Publishing
Full-color photos and step-by-step instructions make recipes easy to navigate. (See also *I'm the Chef: The Young Chef's Chinese Cookbook* by the same publisher.)

Pretend Soup and Other Real Recipes by Molly Katzen and Ann Henderson
This cookbook for children features charming illustrations, step-by-step recipes, and humorous reviews from young food "critics." (See also *Salad People* by Molly Katzen.)

Folktales, Fables, Legends, and Storytelling

Anansi and the Talking Melon by Eric A. Kimmel
Anansi, the trickster spider, convinces elephant and the other animals that a melon can talk.

Bringing the Rain to Kapiti Plain retold by Verna Aardema
A cumulative rhyme tells how Ki-pat brought rain to the drought-stricken Kapiti Plain.

Favorite Folktales from Around the World edited by Jane Yolen
This collection includes 160 tales from over 40 cultures and traditions.

Grandmother Spider Brings the Sun by Geri Keams
A Navajo storyteller tells the Cherokee story of how Grandmother Spider brings light to the animals on her side of the world.

Head, Body, Legs: A Story from Liberia retold by Won-Ldy Paye and Margaret H. Lippert
In this creation story, Head, Arms, Body, and Legs learn that they do better when they work together.

How Chipmunk Got His Stripes: A Tale of Bragging and Teasing by Joseph and James Bruchac
In this retelling of a Native American folktale, Bear and Brown Squirrel have a disagreement about whether Bear can stop the sun from rising.

Leola and the Honeybears by Melodye Benson Rosales
In this Southern retelling of *The Three Little Bears,* Leola finds herself in the home of three honeybears.

Señor Cat's Romance and Other Favorite Stories from Latin America retold by Lucía M. González
This is a collection of popular Latin American tales.

Seven Blind Mice by Ed Young
This retelling of the Indian fable incorporates the days of the week, numbers, and colors.

The Talking Eggs: A Folktale from the American South by Robert D. San Souci
In this Southern folktale, kind Blanche helps an old woman who has magical powers and a chicken house full of talking eggs.

Too Much Talk: A West African Folktale by Angela Shelf Medearis
In this retelling of a Ghanian folktale, a farmer, fisher, weaver, and swimmer are startled by a talking yam, a talking fish, a talking cloth, and talking water. (Look for this out-of-print title in libraries.)

Gingerbread Man Variations

Bad Boys Get Cookie! by Margie Palatini
In this retelling, Wolf detectives Willy and Wally plot to catch a clever, runaway cookie.

Can't Catch Me by Ann Hassett
An ice cube intended for a glass of lemonade decides to head for freedom.

Ginger Bear by Mini Grey
A bear-shaped cookie sets out to avoid being eaten in this inventive retelling.

Gingerbread Baby by Jan Brett
When an impatient boy opens the oven too soon, out pops a gingerbread baby, instead of a fully baked boy.

The Gingerbread Cowboy by Janet Squires
When he gets tired of biscuits, a rancher's wife bakes him a gingerbread cowboy.

The Gingerbread Girl by Lisa Campbell Ernst
The gingerbread man's sister follows in her brother's footsteps, but does him better by outsmarting the fox.

The Runaway Rice Cake by Ying Chang Compestine
After chasing the special rice cake that their mother has made to celebrate the Chinese New Year, three brothers share it with an old woman.

The Runaway Tortilla by Eric A. Kimmel
In this southwestern retelling, a sassy tortilla rolls away from her makers—and all who follow—until she meets a crafty coyote.

Stop That Pickle! by Peter Armour
A variety of foods, and a little boy, chase a runaway pickle that doesn't want to be eaten. [featured on a *Between the Lions* episode]

Wordless Books

10 Minutes till Bedtime by Peggy Rathmann
When a boy's home is a popular stop on a nighttime hamster tour, will they be able to see all of the sights before bedtime?

A Boy, a Dog, and a Frog by Mercer Meyer
A boy and his dog spot a frog in the water. Can they use a net to catch him? See also, *A Boy, a Dog, a Frog, and a Friend* and more by this author.

Good Dog, Carl by Alexandra Day
Pictures tell about the adventures of an infant girl and her dog when Mother goes out for the day. (See also *Carl's Birthday, Carl Goes to Daycare,* and other books about Carl by the same author.)

The Last Laugh by Ariane Dewey and Jose Aruego
A sneaky snake learns "what goes around comes around" in this hilarious fable told with just three words.

Pancakes for Breakfast by Tomie dePaola
Find out what happens when you want pancakes for breakfast but are missing key ingredients—and you live in a house full of mischievous pets.

The Red Book by Barbara Lehman
When a young girl opens a book she finds in the snow, it takes her on a voyage to an island where she meets a new friend.

The Snowman by Raymond Briggs
A snowman comes to life and flies.

Sunlight by Jan Ormerod
As the first rays of sun enter her room, a girl wakes up and starts her day. See also *Moonlight* by the same author.

Tuesday by David Wiesner
In this wordless story, frogs rise on their lily pads and float through the air.

Index by Age

Index by Theme

Index of Children's Books

Index